PRAIS

"I am extremely confident that after reading this book and applying these principles to your life, you'll find a more direct path to making your passion your paycheck."
- Eric Hutcherson, EVP, Chief People and Inclusion Officer,
Universal Music Group

"What I love about *Genius Factor* is that it provides a platform for people to find their sweet spot at the intersection of their passion, talents and career."
- Detavio Samuels, CEO, REVOLT TV

"Make your passion your paycheck is empowering students and adults across the country to develop a personal playbook for success in college, career and life."
- Sterling Roberson, Former VP Career & Technical Education, United Federation of Teachers

"What's brilliant about Torrance's book is that it celebrates everyone's EQ/genius and encourages individuals to figure out how to make work and play one."
- Molly DeWolf Swenson, Investor, Head of Global Partnerships, Community.com

"Make your passion your paycheck is giving individuals the courage and framework to continue pursuing their dreams."
- Pete Chatmon, Writer | Director

"Your pursuit reveals your passion, and the Genius Factor movement is inspiring people all over the globe to make their passion their paycheck."
- Justin Byrd, President Team Velocity

Torrance Hampton

MAKE YOUR PASSION YOUR PAYCHECK ™

GENIUS

MAKE YOUR **PASSION**

YOUR **PAYCHECK**

FACTOR

TORRANCE HAMPTON
with Christina Morgan

GENIUS FACTOR
Copyright © 2022 Torrance Hampton
All rights reserved.

Published by Publish Your Gift®
An imprint of Purposely Created Publishing Group, LLC

Scriptures marked NIV are taken from the New International Version®. Copyright © 1973, 1978, 1984, 2011 by Biblica, Inc.™. All rights reserved.

Printed in the United States of America

ISBN: 978-1-64484-546-2 (print)
ISBN: 978-1-64484-547-9 (ebook)

Gen·ius Fac·tor
/ˈjēnyəs /ˈfaktər/

noun

1. the passions, emotions and energy that influence intelligence aka the factors that make up your genius.

I believe everyone has genius level talent and it's my life's mission to inspire every individual on the planet to discover their Genius Factor and Make Their Passion Their Paycheck.

- Torrance Hampton

MARGIE N. HAMPTON

This book is dedicated to my mother, Margie N. Hampton, who unfortunately lost her battle to breast cancer at age fifty-two. Her passing is one hundred precent the reason I wrote this book and is the catalyst for discovering my passion and genius factor, prioritizing my happiness, and chasing greatness as a serial entrepreneur.

Mom, I love you, I miss you, and I pray this book is a blessing to the world just like you were to our family!

Love Always,
T

Torrance Hampton

Table of Contents

Foreword by Eric Hutcherson, Executive Vice President, Chief People and Inclusion Officer at Universal Music Group xiii

Part I: How I Made My Passion My Paycheck 1
Chapter I. Introduction: Why I Wrote This Book 3
Chapter II. The Genius Factor Communities: What Are They? 5
Chapter III. My Journey: The Torrance Hampton Story 7

Part II: Finding Your Genius Factor: The Playbook 21
Chapter IV. The Importance of EQ-Emotional Intelligence 23
Chapter V. The Genius Factor Success Methodology 27
Chapter VI. Genius Factor Discovery 31
Chapter VII. Genius Factor Mapping: Join Your Community & Passion to Paycheck Profiles 43
Chapter VIII. Genius Factor Activation: The Playbook 95
Chapter IX. Parting Thoughts 109
Acknowledgements 111
Works Cited 115
About the Authors 123

Torrance Hampton

Foreword by Eric Hutcherson, Executive Vice President, Chief People and Inclusion Officer at Universal Music Group

When I graduated from college, I had a choice of two very different career paths. I could either play professional basketball in Australia or enroll in the University of Massachusetts, Amherst sports management master's degree program. Even though it's challenging for most athletes to admit that their playing days are over, I had really decided my path four years earlier. At that time, I chose to attend New York University, which is focused on academics more so than sports, over any of the Division I schools that had offered me a basketball scholarship.

Deep down, I knew I was good, but not that good. None of the Division I schools measured up to NYU academically, and because I wasn't in the top 1 percent of high school basketball players who'd end up playing in the NBA, studying political science as a student athlete at NYU for four years was a more logical choice. However, it was really tough being in this position once again. Do I choose basketball or academics?

The lure of getting paid to play basketball overseas was tempting. But the University of Massachusetts was only accepting thirty students. If I didn't enroll, I'd miss the opportunity.

I told my father about my dream of playing professionally overseas and he shot me a look.

"Son, what are you going to do? I know you're going to make the right decision," he said.

I knew what that meant.

What I didn't know at the time was that by utilizing the process of self-awareness, I was able to make the best decision for myself. In the following pages of *Genius Factor: Make Your Passion Your Paycheck,* written by my dear friend

Foreword

Torrance Hampton, you'll learn to apply this skill to your everyday decision making to make better career choices.

Ultimately, I made the choice to move away from being a career athlete and decided to build my career in the business of sports instead. I'm extremely proud of my decision as I know that I've made a greater impact in my professional career off the court than I would have made on the court.

I attended graduate school with the goal of becoming a sports agent. My first job out of school was in the public relations department at the Boston Celtics before moving to the marketing department of Foot Locker and finally to my dream of working for an agency and representing players.

As a sports agent, your job is not just to negotiate contracts, but to make sure your client is cared for and doing well in every way, and I quickly learned how intense and brutal the world of a sports agent could be. I found myself in repeat scenarios where I was trying to get players to think about their long-term game plan when they were more focused on their present. Imagine trying to convince a pro athlete that he shouldn't buy five different luxury cars in five different colors and should instead buy the dealership. Now think about that as part of your daily routine. I knew I wanted to do more, but I wasn't quite sure what that was. Whatever it was, it would be in the same vein of helping people carve out their future.

Just like when my father knew I had to give up my dream of playing pro sports before I did, my now wife, then fiancée, knew it was time for me to pivot again, this time to the field of human resources. Everyone has a map of where they think they want to be, but sometimes the people in our lives who care most about us can see things we can't. Similar to walking away from my playing days, when I made the decision to no longer be a sports agent it felt like I was walking away from the business of sports as well.

Human resources, historically known as personnel, is the heart of any business or organization. As a human resources professional, you are responsible for the people in the organization and the culture in which they work. Because of who I've always been, this just felt right. The first human resources type job I had was at a company called Inroads, which helped young people of color find internships that led to full-time jobs in corporate America. After having worked with professional athletes, I found that I was really good at working with companies and helping students land the perfect internship. I was so good, in fact, that many of the companies that hired the students with whom I worked offered me a role in their human resources department. I went on to college recruiting and then a few other human resources jobs along the way.

When I became a senior executive at the world's largest human resources consulting firm, Mercer, my passion and paycheck were finally starting to align. I knew I was an excellent human resources professional, and I enjoyed what I did. After working across multiple subsidiaries of Marsh and McLennan, not only did I get the opportunity to work at the pinnacle of my first sporting love, basketball, but I was at the top of my game! I became the chief human resources officer at the National Basketball Association (NBA). Your employer gets to tell you what they feel about you, whether it's through pay, promotions, or the type of assignments they give you. You get to tell them if you agree with their opinion. They don't get to tell you if you should agree with them. When you discover your genius factor, you can decide what path is best for you.

I'm a social genius, which, as you'll learn later in this book, means I'm gifted with the ability to lead and influence others. I believe in a concept I call *hyper networking,* which means your network works for you. I'm constantly connecting with like-minded people because at the end of the day, it's not who you know, really; it's who knows you.

Here's how hyper networking got me to the NBA.

A good friend of mine in the recruiting business happened to have been a high school classmate of a woman who was working as the head of human resources for the NBA. She told my friend she was leaving the NBA, and he recommended me for the job.

I believed if I got the interview, I would get the job. I was on vacation with my family in Florida when I got that initial call that the NBA wanted to talk to me. They offered to postpone the interview for two weeks until I returned, but I immediately told them I'd fly back to New York City the next day. When you're an athlete, you never want to lose an opportunity to get in the game. With that same mindset, I thought to myself that if I waited two weeks, someone else might already be in my spot! I flew back to Florida after the first interview, and I concluded a series of interviews with NBA executives once I returned. Ultimately, I was hired as the chief human resources officer for the National Basketball Association. And I was beyond elated!

At the NBA, I was responsible for the employees and for developing the workplace culture. In addition to the traditional role of a human resources professional, I made it my mission to focus on the employees and create a supportive and collaborative work environment. I wanted our employees to be proud of working for the NBA and to be just as proud of their coworkers. As a member of the executive leadership team, I also played an instrumental role in social initiatives, including the Black Lives Matters movement, and was responsible for supporting the league as we managed through the impact of COVID-19. It's a strange way of thinking about it, but at the League, our most visible "employees" were the players. As they were nearing retirement, many times the players would come to me and say, "My playing days are ending, I need help with what to do next." I had come full circle. Twenty years after trying as a young sports agent to get players to think long term, players were finally seeking my advice about building and shaping their future. NBA players were often uncertain about pursuing a career outside of basketball. I reminded them that no one had a greater work ethic or knew how to sacrifice for the greater good and perform under pressure more than a professional athlete. Just because someone is a famous multi-millionaire doesn't mean they don't face the same insecurities and doubts about the future like the rest of us.

In my current role as the executive vice president, chief people and inclusion officer at Universal Music Group (UMG), I have the ability to positively impact even more people. My role is not different, but the industry and platforms are. Because everyone in the world listens to some form of music, UMG—the home of Drake, Taylor Swift, Kendrick Lamar, Justin Bieber, Billie Eilish, The Weeknd, and more—gives me an even greater opportunity to help people maximize their personal and professional lives and to change the world from the seat in which I sit.

It's been an unexpected but fulfilling journey from the moment my dad looked me in the eyes until now. The decisions that I have made along the way were based on me tapping into my self-awareness (for example, trusting my instinct that pro ball wasn't the direction in which I should go) and prioritizing jobs that allowed me to be passionate about my work and helping others. I am confident that after finishing this book and applying these lessons to your life, you'll be more confident in your decision-making and find a more direct path to making your passion your paycheck!

Torrance Hampton

How I Made
My Passion

I·······················▶

My Paycheck

 There are two options in life that result in increased wisdom, mistakes and mentors.

1

Introduction:
Why I Wrote This Book

I believe that all eight billion people on the planet have genius-level talent. The challenge comes in identifying your specific genius and activating it in your everyday life. Until you do this, you are destined for unhappiness, and trust me, that is a terrible way to live! I know firsthand because it took me twenty years of trial and error to figure out what I was passionate about. I remember feeling unfulfilled and extremely unhappy during high school, college, and working in corporate America. Sound familiar? Of course it does.

I wrote *Genius Factor* because I "cracked the code" for helping individuals achieve happiness in their career. After you discover your passion and talents and activate your genius factor, you'll find that happiness lives where work and play are one! I am a genius, you are a genius, and all eight billion people on the planet are geniuses too.

At different points in our lives, we may feel lost, with no sense of direction. Without a sense of purpose or a clear career path, we feel trapped. That ends today! You are one hundred percent in control of your life, and this book will provide the step-by-step playbook to achieve career happiness and give you the courage to get started. Most people allow the world to happen to them; I believe the most successful people in life go out and happen to the world.

It wasn't until I discovered my genius and started perfecting my craft as a storyteller—executive producing and directing amazing content, broadcast TV commercials, episodic series, documentaries, and films through the production company I founded, G|FACTOR FILMS—that I truly felt professionally satisfied and happy. After finding great success in business, I'm now prioritizing helping the next generation discover their genius and make their passion their paycheck.

Proverbs 18:16 NIV
A gift opens the way and ushers the giver into the presence of the great.

The Genius Factor Communities:
What Are They?

I believe the most important thing that successful people do in life is love what they do. It is unlikely you will find success doing something you hate! Having said that, it's important that I manage your expectations throughout this process. You will need to deploy incredible patience and get excited about the process, the work, and the grind. There is absolutely no shortcut for putting in the work. "The only time success comes before work is in the dictionary," said Vince Lombardi, and there is no magic trick to make this happen overnight.

Now, on to the discovering your "genius" part. If you ask most people if they think they are a genius, they'd probably answer no. And why would anybody answer yes? Apart from sounding like you are on a Kanye rant, the word "genius" brings up larger-than-life figures such as Albert Einstein, Jay-Z, Elon Musk, or Oprah Winfrey. Let's face it, most of us won't end up as household names, and if anyone accepts a genius label, it's usually because the outside world has graciously given them that title.

I am totally challenging that construct, as I believe that everyone has their own God-given talents and genius that can be unleashed. Once you identify your genius, you'll be set on a path to doing what you were put on this Earth to do. You will begin to have a sense of purpose, and that's an incredibly amazing feeling!

As I share the Torrance Hampton journey to discovering, mapping, and activating my genius, I will highlight nine foundational genius factor communities that I identified as part of the Genius Factor Success Methodology. As background, I define *Genius Factor* as the passions, emotions, and energy that influence intelligence—in other words, the factors that make up your genius. These communities I've identified are categories that are strategically aligned to the dominant emotional intelligence (EQ) character traits within all human beings. The nine genius factor communities are as follows:

1. Musical Genius: individuals who are gifted singers, musicians, and composers

2. Athletic Genius: individuals who are athletically and physically gifted

3. Visual Genius: individuals who are gifted in the visual arts

4. Social Genius: individuals who are gifted with the ability to lead and influence others

5. Tech Genius: individuals who are gifted with the ability to develop problem solving software, hardware, and gaming solutions

6. Number Genius: individuals who are gifted in math, science, logic, and reasoning

7. Eco Genius: individuals who are gifted with love and appreciation for the Earth, animals, and all parts of nature

8. Word Genius: individuals who are gifted with the ability to communicate through the written word

9. Spiritual Genius: individuals who are gifted with a higher calling beyond the material world

By the end of this book my goal is for you to have a clear understanding of your genius factor and then to develop a playbook to activate it in your day-to-day life. Let's go!

My Journey:
The Torrance Hampton Story

Soperton, Georgia—population 3,115, would not seem the likeliest catalyst to plant the seed of entrepreneurialism in a young hustler from the DMV (DC, Maryland, Virginia), but for me, it was. Approximately two hours southeast of Atlanta, Soperton is the definition of a "podunk town," but it was home to the first successful business owner for whom I ever worked—my maternal grandfather, Thomas Clarence Little, aka "Papa T.C."

Papa T.C. was a handsome, well-spoken, and hardworking family man. He owned a successful construction/masonry company, and every summer from age five to twelve years old, I worked with him on job sites all over Georgia, and he treated me like one of the fellas on the crew. Bricklaying in 100-degree South Georgia heat and humidity might not sound like much fun, but I loved it! I did odd jobs like grabbing bricks, mortar boards, and wheelbarrows of sand; striking bricks, and even getting lunch for the guys. Papa T.C. paid me for whatever work I did. I used the money I earned to buy whatever I wanted, from video games at Toys R Us to sneakers at Foot Locker.

His wife, my grandmother Ray Helen Little, aka "Ma Ma Ray", ran a beauty salon; she and Papa T.C. were pillars of the community. Papa T.C. was a church deacon and city leader who was passionate about his family and the town of Soperton. They lived in one of the larger houses in town, which he built himself, and they were considered by most as an upper-middle class black family. I was blessed to be exposed to this early example of the advantages of entrepreneurship. As I got older and was on the cusp of being a teenager, bricklaying was no longer "cool" in my mind, and I needed to find a way to make money at home in Northern Virginia. My motivation was probably the same as millions of young boys across the country in 1989—my first pair of Jordans, the Air Jordan IV OG White/Cement. Real talk, I had to get 'em!

My father, my hero, Tommy L. Hampton, was born in Thompson, Georgia, but grew up in the ATL—the amazing city of Atlanta. He was one of nine kids, and his family was dirt poor. But he was extremely motivated and hungry to build a better life for his future family. As a result, he was the first and only in his family to graduate from college—Clark Atlanta University. After graduating, he decided to pursue a career in law enforcement and was blessed to be part of an exclusive group of African American Secret Service agents recruited to join the agency in the early 1970s. This trailblazing group of black agents set the historic course for a much-needed diversity and inclusion initiative for the Secret Service. My dad had an amazing twenty-year career with the Secret Service, visited all seven continents and over three-hundred cities (domestic and international) and protected heads of state and presidents. He also held leadership roles with former President George H.W. Bush and was special agent in charge of the protective detail for First Lady Barbara Bush. Like I said, his career was unreal, and it exposed my family to incredible opportunities that significantly shaped me. He met my mother, Margie N. Hampton, in college, and together they were an amazing team. My mother was one hundred percent the rock of the Hampton household—a devout Christian woman, a loving wife and mother, an amazing cook (I mean, homegirl could burn in the kitchen and cooked everything from scratch), and most importantly, a wonderful support system for our family. Together, my parents raised three beautiful, healthy, and intelligent children (Torrance, Chad, and Mia) while my mom worked both as a social worker part time and in our church with the Stephens' Ministry, a one-on-one spiritual counseling program for parishioners. We were definitely an extremely blessed middle-class black family, but to be clear, we were not rich!

Having said that for context, now let's circle back to the super dope Jordan IV's. There was absolutely no way my dad was going to pony up one hundred dollars plus for a pair of sneakers. So, when I asked him, he said, "Absolutely not!" but offered to pay half if I paid the balance. Initially, I wasn't happy about that counteroffer, but I quickly realized it was fair, and I came to appreciate that amazing life lesson he taught me—you have to be willing to work hard to get the things you want in life. So, I started thinking about ways to make money, and I thought about my grandfather's construction business in Georgia. I definitely was not trying to be a brick mason, but I could explore other service-oriented businesses. My grandfather and father had instilled in me taking pride in a job well done, from laying brick to protecting The President of the United States of America; and at twelve years old, I took pride in doing an excellent job cutting grass at our home. So, why couldn't I cut all my neighbors' grass and get paid in the process? There was another kid in the neighborhood who already offered a lawn cutting service, but his service was sloppy, and he got a little lazy without any competition. So, when he went on vacation, I took advantage of the market and offered to cut lawns for twenty dollars a pop, undercutting his price, and providing a better service and value to my clients—another great lesson I still use today in business. It was an excellent strategy, and it worked extremely well. Within a few months, I was earning three to four hundred dollars per month. I made more than enough to buy my favorite pair of J's (Air Jordan IV – OG White/Cement, to this day still my favorite Jordan silhouette). This was the catalyst for me becoming a quasi-hypebeast, a future sneaker head, and most importantly, an entrepreneur.

I loved making money and the autonomy being an entrepreneur afforded me. However, my parents were both college graduates, and education was always front and center in the Hampton household. Traditional academics were a struggle for me from a very early age. I remember dreading schoolwork as early as the fifth grade. I didn't read or comprehend as quickly and easily as other students, and often, I found schoolwork was just plain boring. I honestly didn't care about George Washington, Saturn, and geometry; it was whatever to me. Neither my younger brother—who tested at near genius level IQ (true story) and is now an amazing orthopedic surgeon—nor my baby sister, now a successful management consultant, struggled academically. I, on the other hand, had to work very hard to be a B-/C+ student, and I was primarily motivated to make an effort in school so I could keep playing sports. As a kid, I played soccer, football, and basketball, which was my true love. I dreamed of playing in the NBA one day. Mercifully, that dream was dashed early in my freshman year of high school when I didn't make varsity, but I still did my thing lettering my junior and senior year, averaging fifteen points and ten rebounds per game, a double-double. Not bad if I say so myself! For me, not going to college for me wasn't an option, and my mother and father were strong advocates of Historically Black Colleges and Universities (HBCUs), since they both attended Clark Atlanta University. My father, being the careful planner that he was, made sure that each of his children were spaced four years apart so he would only be responsible for paying for one child's tuition at a time with no overlap (classic Tommy Hampton).

I was happy to enroll in Morehouse College, aka Da House, in the fall of 1994. If I hadn't been immune to the pop culture influence of Michael Jordan, I for sure wasn't immune to the influence of *The Cosby Show* and the spinoff, *A Different World*. It was amazing to see a functional, middle-class, black family on television once a week, and *A Different World* glamorized the HBCU experience. Plus, as I have come to realize, I was attracted to Morehouse because of its reputation for developing transcendent leaders and churning out legendary alumni like Dr. Martin Luther King Jr. So, with my natural affinity for the ATL, the influence of the fictitious Dr. Heathcliff Huxtable combined with the real-life doctors in my family—my uncles Dr. Chester Little and Dr. Randall Little, who were dentists in Atlanta—I planned to major in biology as a pre-medical student.

I tried to reach my goal of becoming a doctor, but I struggled with the sciences. And truthfully, I had *zero* passion for the profession, I was just attracted to the perceived prestige and money involved. A medical internship in Cleveland, Ohio at Case Western Reserve University School of Medicine the summer before my senior year sealed my fate as a future physician. It was crazy hot and humid all summer in Cleveland, and I was absolutely miserable. I hated dealing with the cadavers, the classes, studying—I hated everything. It was a terrible eight weeks, and at the end of it, I knew I'd never be a doctor or a dentist.

What I liked most about college other than Spelman women—shoutout to the beautiful and intelligent ladies of Spelman College—was hustling and making money. I sold t-shirts on the yard during Morehouse homecoming football games and worked as a valet at Lenox Mall in Buckhead on the weekends. In the mid 90s, Atlanta was quickly turning into the South's entertainment capital, and stars like Outkast, TLC, Usher, Babyface, L.A. Reid, Jazzy Pha, Chris Hicks, Dallas Austin, and Jermaine Dupri were regulars at Lenox Mall. I easily pocketed five hundred dollars on the weekends parking cars at the mall. Even though it was too late to change my course of study completely, I did pivot and started taking business classes during my senior year at "Da House" and loved it.

Good Corporate. Bad Corporate.

After graduating from Morehouse in the summer of 1998, I did what most college students do—I got a job in corporate America. I worked at Xerox selling fax machines and copiers to hospitals and businesses in Washington, DC. Xerox was a tremendous training ground, and I truly learned Sales 101 there. I also met some amazing people who served as mentors and friends and had a tremendous impact on my life, including Frank Edmonds, Al Byrd, Sr. Dan Gillison, Kevin Warren, George Charles (God rest his soul), Douglass Barrios, Chekeim Wymes, Wayne Corion, Rick Levine, Kamonte McCray, Dave Cohen, Scarla Gilbert, Fulton and Chris Bridges, Anita Echols, Rick Torrence, and Craig Buckson. I did well at Xerox, but selling copiers isn't the sexiest thing in the world, and again, I had zero passion for explaining copier speeds and collating features to clients #SMDH. So, what next? I did what most smart people do after tapping out in a corporate job; I moved to another corporate job. This time, it was the software and database giant Oracle. Oracle was a fantastic experience, and I did extremely well there. Software sales was and will always be a great industry, and I was twenty-four-years-old making really good coin! Again, I was blessed to work with some amazing and talented people at Oracle, including Django Degree, Reginia Brown-Hester, Reggie Brown, Valeria Chase-Roberts, Elander Lewis, Richard Dunn, Ryan Nelson and Chris Moore. I purchased my first condo in Reston, Virginia and got a new Honda Accord 4D EX—black/black with a tint (joint was hard). By every outside measure, I was successful, but I wasn't happy. I really didn't like or have any interest in selling copiers or software. I wanted to sell my own stuff—something I was passionate about.

One night, I was lifting weights in my basement with my good friend Bill Dennis. Bill is a very talented creative professional, both a graphic and fashion designer, and like me, he had an affinity for all things lifestyle: music, sports, technology, cars, and fashion. In our youthful ambition, I along with Bill, Danielle Silverstein, and our fourth partner, Caleb "Kaikor" Sawyer, an investor and advisor, decided to start a clothing line.

I named it Ecnorrot. That's right, my name backwards (I admit slightly narcissistic), and I figured it was a great ode to Lady "O"—Oprah/Harpo!

Ecnorrot was a casual urban menswear line inspired by successful companies such as Phat Farm, Akademiks, LRG, Sean Jean, and Ecko Unlimited, and we had a blast putting it together. My family thought I was nuts. And maybe I was, but for the first time in my adult working life, I found something I was passionate about. I hadn't coined my tagline yet, but I was seriously trying to "make my passion my paycheck."

My partners and I had very little success with the brand. A couple of "mom and pop" urban streetwear stores placed orders in DC and Atlanta, and we had a nice feature with a few rappers rocking our clothes in music videos and *XXL* Magazine. But the space was extremely crowded, and we were severely undercapitalized. I didn't know what I was doing, and as a result, it failed miserably. On top of all that, the product wasn't designed well. We designed for what we wanted, not seriously considering the real marketplace opportunity—the rest of the country.

Teachable Moments

First, failure is not a loss. It is simply success turned inside out, and I learned a tremendous amount about myself running Ecnorrot: my hunger, my grit, my hustle, my faith—the stuff that can't be taught in business school!

Second, your passion is one hundred percent where you start in creating a business, but it's not enough to make it successful. You must have a solid business plan with a clear understanding of your value proposition and how your product/service fits into the marketplace. What problem are you solving with this product/service, and how is it uniquely different from the competition? Remember, you will only be paid for the problems that you solve, and if your product/service is not solving a problem, you will not make money.

Third, cash flow is the number one killer of any startup business. You must be properly capitalized; twenty percent of new businesses fail in the first year with fifty percent of new businesses failing by the fifth year. "Cash is king" is cliché but one hundred percent true.

Fourth, you must have a clear, defined strategy to monetize your product/service. This is paramount to the success of the business and most importantly cash flow. It is a hobby until you start making money. #FACTS

Fifth, it's always better to test the marketplace with a minimum viable product (MVP) or beta version of the product/service and use those insights to pivot, iterate, and improve the product/service. It's a huge mistake to build the so-called "perfect" version of your product/service and not test it with real people along the way.

All successful entrepreneurs fail multiple times before they find success—there is no shame there. My disappointment was only compounded by my mother's cancer diagnosis. It was a very difficult time in my professional and personal life, and mom's cancer took it over the top—it was suffocating. She fought the disease hard for five years, but unfortunately, the Lord called her home in October 2003. She was fifty-two years old when she passed. I'll say it again: fifty-two. At twenty-seven years old, you usually aren't forced to think about and face your mortality, but I was. Mom's death definitely hit my reset button, and God used her passing to get my attention. It worked! It forced me to drill down and be more accountable to the Creator and His influence over my life. It also forced me to grow spiritually and took my belief and faith to another level. Tragedy has a way of doing that. When the Lord wants to get your attention, He'll put you in a situation that you can't get out of without His supernatural favor, and that requires acknowledging Him as your one and only source and supply. After a lot of prayer, meditation, counseling, and some extensive soul searching, I was finally able to hone in on my passion and locate my genius factor. My mom's passing served as an amazingly powerful catalyst for discovering my genius and set me on the path of making my passion my paycheck

But before I finally found a fulfilling work life, I headed back to what I knew—corporate America. I sold software yet again, but this time it was business intelligence software for a small startup called Clareos. My boss at the time, Steve Williams, was a supercool dude who to this day is one of the most talented sales professionals I've ever met. He gave me a job when I needed one, and I truly appreciated the opportunity, not to mention, he got me back playing golf on the regular. However, my entrepreneurial instinct remained as strong as ever. I have always wanted to chase my dreams of building successful businesses, and I had a fantastic model of a successful entrepreneur in my grandfather. My goal has always been to create generational wealth and leave a legacy for my children. But you'll have to decide for yourself how important that is for your own life. To me, it was obviously a no-brainer!

In the early 2000s, it was still the wild west for mobile phones, and I believed the mobile phone industry was a great business sector. It made sense to me because I wanted to start another business, but it couldn't be a startup. It needed to be in an established industry that had in-demand products, and cell phones were definitely that. In 2003, Nextel was on the cutting edge of pop culture with their "push to talk, aka chirp" feature being used everywhere, from construction sites to hip-hop videos. Nextel also had an authorized dealer program that was a quasi-franchising model. So, the venture felt very entrepreneurial but still had the advantage of a major established and successful brand. I took the idea to a dear friend of mine, Washington, DC real estate developer Christopher Harrison, and we opened our first Nextel-authorized dealer store in Charlottesville, home to his alma mater, University of Virginia.

In the pre-iPhone world, people were still purchasing their first cell phones, and our store did well. While operating in Charlottesville, we identified a major insight. Being close to a major university campus was a great economic driver of store traffic and sales—we just needed to reproduce the model in a larger city. In

2005, Sprint bought Nextel, and we were able to open two more stores in Richmond, (one on Virginia Commonwealth University's campus), this was around the time that Blackberry was hot and dominating the personal digital assistant market. An extra bonus was that my fiancée (now my lovely wife) got a job at Virginia Commonwealth University, so the expansion and move was perfect. Our VCU Sprint store crushed it, and a major factor was our use of social media marketing. Facebook premiered in 2003 and opened up to all college students nationwide shortly after. All of my sales representatives were active on VCU's campus and Facebook, so every promotion we put on social media hit it out of the park. We started a Facebook campaign called "Blackberry Campus" where we gave away Blackberrys via social platforms, and it went viral. Both Blackberry and Sprint corporate took notice, and our playbook for social media marketing became a part of the "best practices" for other regional Sprint stores. Our stores were ahead of the curve in using social media. Quickly, I also realized we were better at executing hyper-local and creative social media brand marketing than Sprint corporate—a crucial insight that ultimately led to me realizing my dream career.

Things were working pretty well until 2008 rolled around. On top of the cellphone market becoming saturated, the *entire economy crashed*. Credit lines dried up; Sprint had major layoffs, cut authorized dealer commissions by thirty percent, and ultimately, we were forced to sell the business for the best offer available at the time. Since we didn't have a good exit strategy, we were forced to damn near give the business away.

Teachable Moments

1. **Have an exit strategy before you start your business venture.** Whether it is a topline revenue, earnings before interest, taxes, depreciation, and amortization (EBITDA) target, or a date in the future, there should always be a smart yet realistic plan to get out.

2. **Study industry trends.** You must be a student of your business and your industry. If I had done better market research, I would have known

the cellular industry wasn't going to trend up forever and was actually trending flat, which is the step before trending down.

Having said that, if I had a better exit strategy, I would have been actively looking at trends twelve months before the economic crash and sold much earlier to a larger dealer group at a significantly higher price point. Again, you never really fail; you just learn, but sometimes at a painful cost!

3. **Always have a side hustle.** I was saved financially, in part, by my side hustle. I was also buying and flipping residential real estate with my friend Kaikor Sawyer. Kaikor also helped with operations in the Sprint business, and we started a real estate renovation business on the side in Richmond. We found old, rundown homes and brought them back to brilliance. We did well, however, life happened. By this time, my wife and I had our first child, London, on the way. Like in most households, bills were due on the first and fifteenth of the month, and the Mrs. wasn't keen on another entrepreneurial plunge. Bottom line, I needed a job—again!

As fate would have it, a mutual friend, Randy Dillard, introduced me to Kenneth Johnson, founder and CEO of Johnson, Inc., a prominent marketing, branding, and communication firm headquartered in Richmond. Ken and I had a real conversation in our initial meeting, and I told him where I was, and he then told me, "T, you need a job, my brother, and I'd like to hire you here at Johnson, Inc." He hired me on the spot, and Johnson, Inc. turned out to be the perfect job for me, which came at the perfect time. Praise God! I prayed for an opportunity to work on the branding and marketing strategy side of the business because I was tired of selling widgets, i.e., Xerox-copiers, Oracle-software, and Sprint cell phones. I knew I was smart and creative enough to work with brands as a strategic thinking partner, helping them craft brand marketing strategies and execution. Most importantly, I felt passionate about it. Johnson, Inc. provided a unique opportunity, had some amazing existing clients, and also produced live events as an experiential marketing agency. I had the opportunity to work with some incredible brands, including BMW, the Virginia Tourism Corporation (aka Virginia Is for Lovers), and the Barclays Center in Brooklyn, New York. As a result, I also learned the live event activation business. I was mastering the technical aspects of corporate marketing, the importance of strategic thinking and planning, and the ability to execute on behalf of the brand at live events.

Johnson, Inc. was and still is a special place and a very entrepreneurial environment. For the first time in my professional career, going to the office didn't feel like work. I was excited and passionate about what I was doing and got a chance to work on branded content with our strategic partners. In the spring 2013, Johnson, Inc. launched *RVA Grooves: All Things Arts & Culture*. *RVA Grooves* was a hyper-local TV show hosted by social entrepreneur and restauranteur Kelli Lemon that showcased the emerging musical arts, visual arts, and culinary arts scene in Richmond. Ken developed the idea, served as executive producer, and allowed me to run with it as producer and director. The thirty-minute show aired on the NBC Richmond affiliate station NBC12, and we successfully produced eighteen episodes over two seasons. This is when it all came together for me—my pinnacle genius factor moment. The moment I fell in love with storytelling. I absolutely loved the storytelling process and the process of learning how to direct and produce branded content. It didn't feel like work and was a tremendous amount of fun. I loved it! I now knew I wanted to be a professional storyteller and help brands influence their target audience in the most effective ways possible. I cemented what I wanted to do after I worked as a producer/director on *RVA Grooves* and directed the RVA (Richmond, VA) "Happy" video. In 2014, people all over the world remade their own video version of Pharrell William's hit song to highlight their city. I remember directing a scene for the *RVA* "Happy" Pharrell Williams remake video at Richmond's Saint Paul's Baptist Church. This specific scene was a remake of the church scene in the original "Happy" video, and the entire Saint Paul's choir (two hundred members) was rocking out and singing the hook, "Clap along if you feel like a room without a roof." We shot three separate takes where the choir performed the entire song (it sounded amazing), and in between the second and third takes, I stood in front of the pulpit looking at Pastor Lance Watson and the choir and thanked God for this unreal opportunity. It was an incredible feeling, and in that very moment, I said a quick gratitude prayer and told myself, "This isn't work; I'm passionate about storytelling and will direct and produce amazing stories and make a great living doing it!" Over the next two years, I continued to improve my producing and directing chops and totally committed to the goal of directing broadcast TV commercials for Fortune 500 brands and eventually feature films.

In May 2016, I left Johnson, Inc. and founded G|FACTOR FILMS, and I have the entire Johnson, Inc. family to thank for creating the perfect season for Torrance Hampton! #GRATEFUL

My Greatest Chapter

The seasons of your life will drastically change every time you decide to step out on faith.

Faith: Believing in advance what will only make sense in reverse. Yeah, that one hits different, right? That's the Torrance Hampton definition of faith, and starting a business without knowing when and/or where I would get my first client qualifies as stepping out on faith. So, of course, I did what I do best. I bet on myself and my work ethic. As my dear friend and mentor Eric Hutcherson—EVP Chief People Officer, Universal Music Group—would say, hyper networking is a major key to professional success. It's not only about who you know, but more importantly who knows you and who's willing to put their name on you. This idea that your network should always be working on your behalf is real, and that mindset had me on the grind working my network. Within thirty days of leaving Johnson, Inc., I had a check for $50,000 from Radio One, a media conglomerate that primarily targets African American consumers. The project had me serving as producer and director for a series of vignettes highlighting a documentary called *Saving Tomorrow Today* sponsored by the University of Phoenix. I got this opportunity because I had a strong relationship with Detavio Samuels, currently the CEO of REVOLT TV, but at that time he was the president of Interactive One, Radio One's, internal advertising and digital content agency. I met Detavio through a very close friend, Justin Byrd, who at the time was the head of multicultural marketing at FCA-Fiat Chrysler Automobiles (Fiat, Chrysler, Dodge, Jeep) and is now the president of Team Velocity, a customer relationship management (CRM) technology platform for the automotive industry.

Throughout my career, I have continued to successfully leverage my network, and that has resulted in a diverse list of clients, including Walt Disney Studios, NFL, NBA, Comcast/NBC Universal, BET, Nickelodeon, Lego, Bentley, Aston Martin, and more. Additionally, I have produced and directed a three-part docuseries titled *Founding in Color*, which is currently on NBC's streaming platform Peacock TV, and several other documentary films, including *Unapologetically BL(VA)CK*, *I Am a Dreamer*, and a featurette behind the scenes short film about Kevin Durant's AppleTV series *Swagger*.

My dominant genius is social genius, which I define as gifted with the ability to influence and communicate with groups of people. Social geniuses tend to have natural leadership skills and excel in professions such as sales and marketing, entrepreneurship, and public speaking. This is totally me! I'm also a visual genius—an individual who is gifted in the visual arts—and this plays out in my life as a storyteller/filmmaker, creative director, executive producer, and director.

The bottom line is, if I had been able to identify my genius factor earlier in life, I truly believe I would have significantly shortened my path to professional success and happiness. I would not have tried to become a medical doctor or sell copiers or cell phones. If I were more corporate-inclined, I would have probably aspired to be the chief marketing officer for a Fortune 500 company. But being dead set on working for myself and creating a legacy for my family, I am on purpose and exactly where I am supposed to be today—founder, creative director, executive producer and director of G|FACTOR FILMS. Most importantly I am privileged to wake up extremely happy on a daily basis, and trust me when I say joyfulness is a gamechanger in life! #FACTS

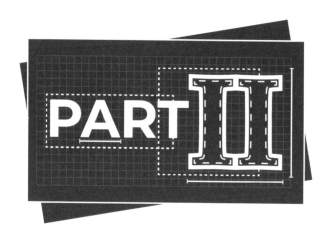

Finding Your
Genius Factor

The Playbook

 The way you predict your future is to create it.

Torrance Hampton

The Importance of EQ-Emotional Intelligence

Around the time that my mother passed away in 2003, I was unemployed, and my clothing line had failed miserably. I was in the depression phase of the grieving process, and while praying heavily for God's guidance and reading anything that could help me navigate this difficult time, I came across a study published by Harvard University psychologist, Dr. Howard Gardener. For those not familiar, Dr. Gardener introduced the theory of multiple intelligences, where he suggests that all human beings have different types of intelligence. As opposed to measuring intelligence quotient (IQ), Dr. Gardener argues we should measure something called emotional intelligence (EQ).

Dr. Gardner's theory directly challenged the standard psychological view of intellect: that there is a single human intelligence for all human beings that is adequately measured by IQ. The idea that IQ is the best measure of intelligence, in my humble opinion, is a completely ridiculous and antiquated concept. In contrast, the theory of multiple intelligences claims that all human beings have a number of different intellectual capacities and intelligences. These types of "intelligences" can be categorized and measured by emotional intelligence (EQ). I fell in love with this concept. It spoke directly to my spirit, and I started drilling down on the theory of multiple intelligences and EQ.

EQ is defined as the ability to understand, use, and manage you own emotions in positive ways. I was totally feeling this definition, which is rooted in self-awareness, a critically important genius factor principle we will cover later. Additionally, Dr. Gardner goes on to categorize the eight types of intelligences as follows:

- Musical Intelligence: Learns through songs, rhythmic and tonal patterns, instruments, and musical expression; gifted in the musical arts

- Bodily/Kinesthetic Intelligence: Learns through bodily interactions with one's environment and using the body movements to express emotions

- Verbal/Linguistic Intelligence: Learns through spoken or written words—reading, listening, speaking, and writing

- Mathematical/Logical Intelligence: Learns through reasoning and problem-solving—numbers and the sciences

- Visual/Spatial Intelligence: Learns visually and organizes ideas spatially; gifted in the visual arts and thinks in terms of colors, images, and pictures

- Intrapersonal Intelligence: Learns through feelings, values, intuition, and innate knowledge of self-reflection

- Interpersonal Intelligence: Learns through communication and interactions with individuals and/or groups of people

- Naturalist Intelligence: Learns through classification, categories, and hierarchies; innate affinity for nature, the environment, and animals

Dr. Gardner also stated that human beings have at least one and often multiple different types of intelligence. After reading about Dr. Gardner's work, I was so inspired that I wanted to spread the gospel of EQ. But who really understands the difference between *intrapersonal intelligence* and *interpersonal intelligence*? I had to make it simple and break it down into words anyone could understand.

To that end, the Genius Factor Success Methodology is inspired by the theory of multiple intelligences and includes nine foundational genius factor communities:

musical genius, athletic genius, visual genius, social genius, tech genius, number genius, eco genius, word genius, and spiritual genius. The communities are categories that strategically align to the dominant EQ character traits within all human beings. I have said it once, and I will say it again: I firmly believe that everyone on the planet is a genius and that everyone has genius-level talent. The challenge is that most individuals have not successfully activated their genius. That's where I come in, and it's my job to help you discover and activate your genius factor with the help of this book.

You must learn to control your emotions, or they will control you. Being clouded by emotional insecurities is a huge vulnerability.

The Genius Factor Success Methodology

The Genius Factor Success Methodology is based on the exact process I went through to discover and activate my genius. I synthesized the most impactful, teachable moments throughout my journey and developed them into a framework. This framework encompasses twenty years of my life and, in my humble opinion, is priceless. I say that with the utmost confidence because if you follow this methodology, it will significantly shorten your pathway to career success and ultimate happiness, and that, my friends, is *priceless*!

The Genius Factor Success Methodology is the basis for the *Make Your Passion Your Paycheck* career exploration course I facilitate at high schools and colleges around the country. I also use this as the foundation for all my workshops and keynote speaking engagements. The course is designed the help young adults (or anyone) unpack thier passion and activate their genius; ultimtely creating alignment with their personal interests and career pathways, so work and play are one. This challenge-based supplemental educational program is focused on developing leadership qualities, college/career readiness, and life skills. The course uses lectures, coaching, and interactive group discussions led by business and education professionals.

Having said that, the three foundational pillars for the Genius Factor Success Methodology are:

#1: *Genius Factor Discovery*

You will discover and identify skills for optimizing your EQ. This pillar is designed to highlight the importance of self-awareness and create clear thinking around internal feelings, motives, and desires.

Learning objectives include: a heightened sense of self-awareness plus an increased understanding of passion and God-given talents.

#2: *Genius Factor Mapping*

You will identify and connect with the genius factor community that best aligns and maps to your passion and talents.

Learning objectives include: mapping dominant EQ character traits around passion and talents to one and/or multiple genius factor communities.

#3: *Genius Factor Activation*

You will develop a customized playbook that provides your passion to paycheck blueprint for activating your genius factor in daily life experiences so work and play are one.

Learning objectives include: developing a clear strategy and activation plan for navigating your genius in day-to-day life and helping accelerate the achievement of key milestones and goals.

People who go through this program are profoundly transformed. You will discover your passion and genius factor, plus develop a playbook for success in college, career, and life where work and play are one. Ultimately, this process is magical and creates unbelievable opportunities for sustained happiness in life. To be clear, this does not mean you are immune to facing challenges in life. You will have multiple. Having said that, you will be able to navigate challenging situations with a sense of purpose and joy, and that's absolutely priceless, which I know first-hand because I'm living it.

This next section is meant to be collaborative and is set up as an active workshop taken directly from my course, *Make Your Passion Your Paycheck*. As you read through each pillar, you should complete the activities before moving on to the next section. Again, this is the exact process I went through, and it totally works if you follow it, so don't cheat yourself by not completing the assignments. Let's get to it!

Genius Factor Discovery
Module #1:
Self Awareness
Know Thyself

Let's start with module number one, which is the most important. In this module, there are three core concepts you must understand before you can move forward: **self-awareness, passion, and talent.** Let's first have an in-depth discussion on self-awareness, which is a critically important skill you must start to master and deploy throughout this process and in life. The best academic definition I found of self-awareness was published in *The Harvard Business Review* (HBR). They divide self-awareness into two types: internal self-awareness and external self-awareness. For the purposes of this book, we will quickly sum up internal self-awareness, which is more useful in the context of this discussion.

Internal Self-Awareness

According to the HBR, internal self-awareness represents how clearly we see our own values, passions, aspirations, fit with our environment, reactions (including thoughts, feelings, behaviors, strengths, and weaknesses), and impact on others. "We have found that internal self-awareness is associated with higher job and relationship satisfaction, personal and social control, and happiness," says Dr. Tasha Eurich.

My definition of self-awareness is simple; you have to *know thyself*. To do that, you must have conscious knowledge of your feelings, motives, and desires. Self-awareness should play a major role in your life and the educational process because it allows you to clarify and focus on exactly what you should be studying, learning, and doing. This section below is taken from the self-awareness audit that is completed when you take my course. This audit is designed for people of all ages who are looking to achieve self-awareness in three foundational life categories: (A) values + goals, (B) personality, and (C) interpersonal relationships. This exercise is extremely important; be honest, instinctive, and thoughtful with all your answers and don't cheat yourself. These questions will help you think through your internal feelings, motives, and desires and ultimately heighten your sense of self-awareness. Without mastering this first step, it's next to impossible to accurately determine your passion. And without that, it is highly unlikely you can align your life to make work and play one.

SELF-AWARENESS AUDIT (A): VALUES + GOALS

1. What do you stand for, or what is your belief system? What values guide your daily life?

_____

_____

_____

2. Rank (in order of priority) the five most important things in your life: Family, Career, Money, Love, Knowledge, Spirituality, etc.

_____

_____

_____

3. What are your ultimate dreams and goals? If money was not an issue, what would you be doing? Short-term (1-5 years) versus Long-term (6-15 years)?

_____

_____

_____

4. Why is achieving your dreams and/or goals so important?

_____

_____

_____

5. What are your biggest obstacles or limiting steps to achieving your dreams?

_____

_____

_____

6. How much time are you dedicating to each goal? Should you be reprioritizing your time based on your dreams?

_____

_____

_____

7. Given only one year to live, how would you spend your time?

_____

_____

_____

SELF-AWARENESS AUDIT (B): PERSONALITY

1. What three words would you use to best describe yourself?

_____

_____

_____

2. What do you love about yourself? Greatest strengths?

_____

_____

_____

3. What are your areas of opportunity? Greatest weaknesses?

_____

_____

_____

4. How do you make decisions? Intuition (gut) or logical analysis?

_____

_____

_____

5. What is your biggest regret? What were the teachable moments from this experience?

_____

_____

_____

6. What are you afraid of? Why do you fear these things?

_____

_____

_____

7. How has your personality changed since your childhood?

_____

_____

_____

SELF-AWARENESS AUDIT (C): RELATIONSHIPS

1. Self-love: How do you practice and reinforce it in your life?

_____

_____

_____

2. Has communication been a strength or weakness in your previous relationships?

_____

_____

_____

3. What are your greatest struggles or areas of opportunity in your relationships (friends, family, or significant other)?

_____

_____

_____

4. Rank the five love languages (listed below) in priority as it relates to you and explain why.
   - **Words of Affirmation:** appreciates complimentary words

_____

_____

_____

   - **Receiving Gifts:** likes to receive thoughtful gifts

_____

_____

_____

   - **Acts of Service:** likes to do kind things for others

_____

_____

_____

   - **Quality Time:** enjoys spending time with loved ones

_____

_____

_____

- **Physical Touch:** enjoys holding hands, hugging, public display of affection (PDA), all physical expressions of love

_____

_____

_____

5. Describe the best and/or special moments of significant relationships (friends, family, or significant other). What made them so special?

_____

_____

_____

6. Describe extremely disappointing moments of significant relationships (friends, family, or significant other). What were the teachable moments?

_____

_____

_____

7. What regrets do you have, if any?

_____

_____

_____

8. If you only had seven minutes left to live, who would you call and what would you say? Why?

_____

_____

_____

Module #2:
Passion—What Motivates You?
Know Your Why

What you like to do is different than what you love to do. For example, when a task becomes difficult, do you work through it or quit? I really liked basketball and thought I loved it. But I wasn't willing to put in the extra work to improve, and I did not have the talent to be great at it like Kobe and Michael.

In contrast, I've always loved shoes, sports, movies, and music. But I never thought or believed in my heart that I could turn my passion for these things into a career. They were just objects. However, when I examined the nexus, the connective tissue that tied everything together, was the story behind the product, otherwise known as storytelling. I absolutely love what I do as a professional storyteller because I help brands tell emotional stories that connect with consumers.

This section below is the passion audit, which is designed to help you determine your why—what you are most passionate about. Passion is super important because if you aren't passionate about it, that means you don't love it. If you don't love it, you are guaranteed to quit when it gets hard, and trust me, it will get hard. Nothing worth having in life comes easy.

 You only qualify for what you pursue, and your past decisions have created your present season.

PASSION AUDIT

1. Where do you find significant moments of joy and happiness?

_____

_____

_____

2. What activities give you the most satisfaction?

_____

_____

_____

3. What excites you about life?

_____

_____

_____

4. What are your hobbies? What does your inner voice say (secret ambitions)?

_____

_____

_____

5. What are your dreams? Describe your dreams in vivid details.

_____

_____

_____

Module #3:
Talent – What Is Your Genius?
My Genius Level Talents Are…

Again, I believe that everyone has innate, God-given talents, or what I call genius. But you have to work to develop that talent into skill. That is the difference between being good and being great. Simply put, hard work always beats talent when talent doesn't work hard.

For example, Kobe Bryant had athletic talent, but he had to work to develop skill. In high school, Kobe was known for hitting the gym two hours before his classes started to get his shots up and work on perfecting his craft. He used that philosophy throughout his whole career in the NBA and put in extra training time to get way better than his competition—a foundation that became the famous Mamba Mentality.

Athletes are easy examples to highlight because you can see their talent on the court, field, or wherever they play. Musicians are great examples too because you can see someone sing well or perform live. Business and other careers are different. Let's take me as an example. As a social and visual genius, it's now apparent to me that even at a young age, I was great at winning over and influencing people. During my first entrepreneurial experience when I started my lawn service at twelve years old, I was able to secure a majority of the neighbors based on my relationships because I was always friendly and kind to people. Therefore, they trusted me to cut their grass and paid me for it. At age twelve, I didn't realize what I was doing, but I was building relationships, an example of my social genius. As an adult, I had to work at developing that into a skill and figure out ways to monetize it consistently.

This section below is the talent audit, which is designed to help you determine and unpack your innate genius level talent/s.

TALENT AUDIT

1. What is your superpower? What comes naturally for you, and what do you do extremely well?

_____

_____

_____

2. What have you excelled at in the past? Where have you been successful in your life?

_____

_____

_____

3. What have other people said you are good at?

_____

_____

_____

4. What are your strengths?

_____

_____

_____

5. What are your weaknesses?

_____

_____

_____

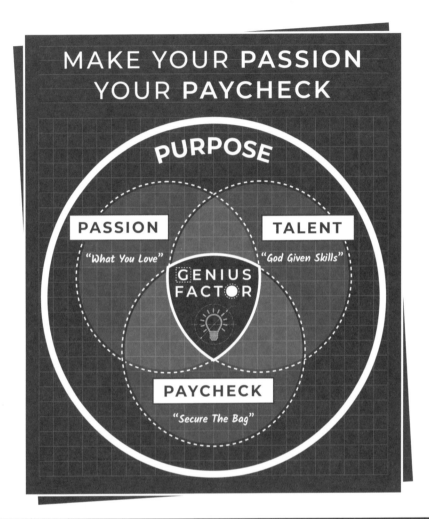

MAKE YOUR PASSION YOUR PAYCHECK

PURPOSE

PASSION
"What You Love"

TALENT
"God Given Skills"

GENIUS FACTOR

PAYCHECK
"Secure The Bag"

Passion gives you the drive to push through difficult times, while purpose ignites the spirit, creating infectious momentum.

Genius Factor Mapping:

Join Your Community & Passion to Paycheck Profiles

This section is designed to help you determine the genius factor community that best aligns and maps to your passion and talents. As you read through each genius factor community, keep yourself honest around your passion, talents, and what you love to do and place a checkmark next to the genius factors that speak to you. As a primer, I've listed examples of how each individual genius factor manifests in the real world today. One question I often get is can you have more than one genius factor? The answer is yes; most people have between one to three, but typically, there is a dominant genius factor in all of us. For example: I am a social genius and a visual genius, but my social genius is my dominant genius factor.

Musical Genius — Individuals who are gifted singers, musicians, and composers.

Musical Geniuses are individuals who are gifted with musical intuition and excel at singing, playing instruments, writing, arranging, and performing musical sequences, musical artists, actors and entertainers, producers, sound engineers, music supervisors and original composers for motion picture film scoring.

 **Athletic** Genius – Individuals who are athletically and physically gifted.

Athletic Geniuses are individuals who are gifted with bodily and kinesthetic intuition and excel as athletes at all levels (youth, collegiate, professional) of all sports, and anyone proficient in other forms of physical exercise i.e. dancers, trainers, martial artists and yoga instructors.

 **Visual** Genius – Individuals who are gifted in the visual arts.

Visual Geniuses are individuals who are artistically gifted such as illustrators, painters, designers, sculptures, architectures, photographers, cinematographers, directors, and culinary artists.

 **Social** Genius – Individuals who are gifted with the ability to lead and influence others.

Social geniuses have excellent leadership and communication skills and often excel as sales/marketing professionals, entrepreneurs, actors, public speakers, attorneys, politicians, networkers/conveners, social media influencers, and socialites.

Tech Genius – Individuals who are gifted with the ability to develop problem-solving software, hardware, and gaming solutions.

Tech geniuses are gifted with the intuition for developing software and hardware solutions and excel as internet technology (IT) professionals, including coders/software developers, software/hardware engineers, cybersecurity engineers, web developers, video game developers, UX/UI developers, and professional gamers.

Number Genius – Individuals who are gifted in mathematics, science, logic, and reasoning.

Number geniuses are gifted with the intuition for developing mathematical and scientific solutions and excel as doctors, mathematicians, scientists, accountants, professors/teachers, analysts, researchers, and economists.

Eco Genius – Individuals who are gifted with the love and appreciation for the Earth, animals, and all parts of nature.

Eco geniuses are gifted with the love and appreciation for the environment and excel as agriculture engineers, civil engineers, veterinarians, horticulturists, ecologists, recycling/sustainability designers, and outdoor adventurers (i.e., those who enjoy camping, hiking, and fishing)

45

Word Genius – Individuals who are gifted with the ability to communicate through the written word.

Word geniuses are gifted with the ability to speak, read, and write and excel as magazine writers/editors, broadcast journalists (news/sports), authors, public speakers, English teachers, literature professors, actors, poets, musicians, screenplay writers, comedians, and all storytellers.

Spiritual Genius – Individuals who are gifted with a higher calling beyond the material world.

Spiritual geniuses are gifted with a self-reflective intuition around a higher calling and purpose and excel as philosophers, strategists, clergy/theologians, psychologists, and mindfulness instructors.

List and prioritize the top three genius factor communities that best align to your passion and talents:

1. _____

2. _____

3. _____

Passion To Paycheck Profiles

Now that you have identified and selected the genius factor communities that best aligns with your passion and talents, we can move to reviewing the passion to paycheck profiles. These profiles will highlight real-life examples of individuals who, in my opinion, are living in their genius factor. This section is meant to be collaborative, so as you review the profiles, make notes based on the genius factor communities that speak to you and that you've prioritized. Also make sure to answer the summary questions at the very end. This section is super fun because you will begin to see yourself and your genius factor revealed within these examples. Enjoy!

Musical Genius

Passion To Paycheck Profiles

Individuals who are gifted singers, musicians, and composers.

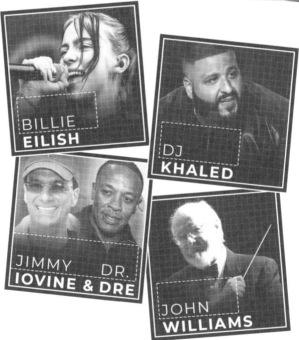

Musical Genius

Passion To Paycheck Profiles

Billie **Eilish**

Goal: Disrupt the pop music scene

Passion: Songwriting

Talent: Singing & Songwriting

In Their Own Words: "I don't know how to function without music. When I'm not making it, I'm listening to it. It gives me courage and takes care of my mind."

Passion to Paycheck: ┝ ‑ ➔

- Joined choir at age eight.
- Wrote her first "real" song at age eleven for her mother's songwriting class.
- Released the song *Ocean Eyes* on SoundCloud in 2015, written and produced by her brother, Finneas, originally written for his band.
- Several major record labels asked to buy the rights for the song. *Ocean Eyes* was released worldwide by Darkroom/Interscope Records in 2016.

Outcome: "Ocean Eyes" became a critical and commercial success and was included on her EP, *Don't Smile at Me*. Her debut studio album, *When We All Fall Asleep, Where Do We Go?*, was released in March 2019. She won five Grammy Awards in 2020 and is considered one of the most influential musicians in the world.

Notes:

Musical Genius
Passion To Paycheck Profiles

DJ **Khaled**

Goal: Become a music producer & executive

Passion: Hip Hop Music

Talent: DJ'ing and producing

In Their Own Words: "I have always been told, 'no,'...And I always took them [sic] 'nos' and turned them into 'yes,'...I always believed in my path, my vision."

Passion to Paycheck: ┠ - ➤

- While still a teenager, Khaled briefly worked at New Orleans's Odyssey record store, networking with rising rap artists like Birdman and Lil Wayne.

- Khaled moved to Miami in 1998 and worked in radio as a cohost of *The Luke Show* with Luther Campbell of 2 Live Crew.

- In 2006, Khaled's debut album entitled *Listennn... the Album*, reached number twelve on the Billboard 200 charts.

- In 2010, Khaled's single *All I Do Is Win*, featuring the likes of Ludacris and Snoop Dogg, went double platinum and reached number six on the Billboard charts.

Outcome: Khaled released his first number one album in *Major Key* in 2016. He continues to collaborate with household names in the music industry and has become a social media star on Snapchat. Khaled has also appeared in films including *Spies in Disguise* and *Bad Boys for Life*.

Notes:

Musical Genius

Passion To Paycheck Profiles

Jimmy **Iovine**

Goal: Become a record executive

Passion: Producing music

Talent: Sound engineering & music production

In Their Own Words: "I didn't have any sophistication...I was just a kid from Brooklyn. But what I learned is the why, the how, the work ethic."

Passion to Paycheck: ┝ ━ ━ ━ ━ ━ ━ ━ ━ ━ ━ ━ ━ ━ ━ ━ ━ ━ ━ ➤

- Began working as a sound engineer for John Lennon and Bruce Springsteen in 1972.
- In 1990 founded Interscope Records and signed Tupac Shakur as one of his first hip-hop artists in 1991.
- Iovine has been involved in the production of over 250 records.
- In 2006, Iovine and Dr. Dre co-founded Beats by Dr. Dre. Apple acquired Beats Electronics in 2014, and Iovine launched what became Apple Music.

Outcome: In 2013. Iovine and Dr. Dre donated $70 million to the University of Southern California to create the USC Jimmy Iovine and Andre Young Academy for Arts, Technology, and the Business of Innovation. Iovine has also been honored by the Producers & Engineers Wing of the Recording Academy. His net worth is estimated at $970 million.

Notes:

Musical Genius

Passion To Paycheck Profiles

Dr. **Dre**

Goal: Become a world class music producer

Passion: Music production

Talent: Sound engineering & music production

In Their Own Words: "There's three types of people in the world: Those who don't know what happened. Those who wonder what happened. And people . . . that make things happen!"

Passion to Paycheck: ┣ ─ ➔

- Inspired by the Grandmaster Flash song *The Adventures of Grandmaster Flash on the Wheels of Steel*, he became a DJ in a local club in LA.

- In 1988, Dr. Dre and the founding members of N.W.A released their first album, Straight Outta Compton.

- Post N.W.A, Dr. Dre produced hits with Death Row Records and founded his own label, Aftermath Entertainment, a division of Interscope Records, where he signed and produced Eminem and 50 Cent.

- Formed Beats by Dre in 2006 with Jimmy Iovine and released the first headphone product in 2008.

Outcome: Dr. Dre earned approximately $52 million from selling part of his share of Aftermath Entertainment to Interscope Records in 2001. He has received twenty-six Grammy nominations and won six. He sold Beats to Apple for $3.2 billion in 2014. His net worth is estimated at $800 million.

Notes:

Musical Genius

Passion To Paycheck Profiles

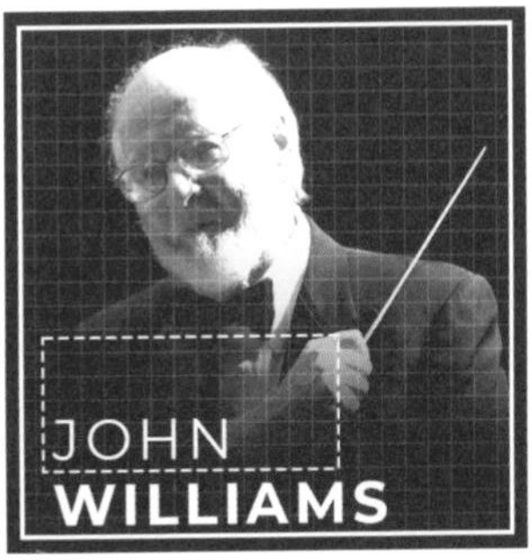

John **Williams**

Goal: Become a world-class composer

Passion: Writing music

Talent: Scoring television and films

In Their Own Words: "As a youngster, I never dreamed there could be a career actually earning a living writing music."

Passion to Paycheck:

- Attended UCLA and studied composition privately with the Italian composer, Mario Castelnuovo-Tedesco, a guitarist and film composer who scored over two hundred films.
- Studied at the Juilliard School in New York while working as a jazz pianist at night and a session musician.
- In 1974, Steven Spielberg approached Williams to compose the music for his feature directorial debut, *The Sugarland Express*. They teamed up again a year later for Spielberg's second film, *Jaws*.
- Williams has won five Oscars for his work on *Fiddler on the Roof, Jaws, Star Wars, E.T.*, and *Schindlers' List*.

Outcome: Williams' iconic film scores also includes music for *Jurassic Park, Raiders of the Lost Ark, Home Alone, Harry Potter, Dear Basketball* by Kobe Bryant, and much more. He is estimated to have a net worth of $300 million.

Notes:

Athletic Genius

Passion To Paycheck Profiles

Individuals who are athletically
and physically gifted.

Athletic Genius
Passion To Paycheck Profiles

Michael **Jordan**

Goal: Become the world's greatest basketball player

Passion: Competitive sports

Talent: Playing basketball

In Their Own Words: "Anything can happen if you are willing to put in the work and remain open to the possibility. Dreams are realized by effort, determination, passion, and staying connected to that sense of who you are."

Passion to Paycheck: ┝ - ➔

- Famously cut from the varsity basketball team as a sophomore in high school but as a junior made varsity and averaged twenty-five points per game, proving he could compete at the next level.

- Hit game-winning shot to win the NCAA Championship in 1982 and named ACC Freshman of the year while attending The University of North Carolina at Chapel Hill.

- Drafted number three overall in 1984 to the Chicago Bulls.

- Voted Rookie of the Year in 1985. The first Air Jordan sneaker (Air Jordan I) with Nike was released the same year.

- Six-time NBA Champion, six-time NBA Finals MVP, fourteen-time NBA All Star, ten-time NBA Scoring Champ, and two-time Olympic Gold Medalist.

Outcome: Michael Jordan's Air Jordan brand is worth an estimated $3 billion, and Jordan has earned over a billion dollars from his Nike deal. In 2010, Jordan became the majority owner of the Charlotte Bobcats, currently the Charlotte Hornets, making him the first former player to be the majority owner of an NBA franchise.

Notes:

_____

_____

Athletic Genius
Passion To Paycheck Profiles

Nicole **Lynn**

Goal: Become a professional sports agent

Passion: Representing professional athletes

Talent: Strategic negotiations

In Their Own Words: "I hope I'm known as someone who is bringing as many people along on the ride with her as she can . . . especially women and minorities."

Passion to Paycheck: ├ – ➔

- Graduated from the University of Oklahoma with a bachelor's in business management and doctor of law (J.D.) with honors.

- Worked on Wall Street briefly, hoping to become a financial advisor for pro athletes, then worked at the NFL Players Union after graduating law school.

- In 2015, Lynn became the first female agent at agency PlayersRep, which was acquired by Lil Wayne's Young Money APAA Sports in 2017.

- Represented Quinnen Williams, the number-three pick in the 2019 NFL draft, who agreed to a four-year deal with the Jets worth $32.5 million featuring a $21.6 million signing bonus.

Outcome: Made history when her client NFL player Quinnen Williams was drafted as a number-three pick for the New York Jets. That move made Lynn the first Black woman in history to represent a top-five pick. Her extensive client list includes NFL players with the Denver Broncos, Oakland Raiders, Washington Redskins; an ESPY-nominated softball star, and a ballerina from American Ballet Theatre. A TV show inspired by her life is in development by 50 Cent and STARZ. Most recently, Lynn joined Klutch Sports Group as senior agent and president of football operations.

Notes:

Athletic Genius
Passion To Paycheck Profiles

Chloe **Kim**

Goal: Become a champion snowboarder

Passion: Snowboarding

Talent: Athletic ability

In Their Own Words: "[I]f you just push through the struggles and the hard times, it'll be so worth it in the end because you will be able to get to your dreams."

Passion to Paycheck: ⊢ − → ➔

- Kim's father, a skiing enthusiast, started her on the snowboard at age four.
- Kim started competing at age six and improved even more after living in Switzerland and joining the Swiss snowboarding team in third grade.
- Earned a silver medal in superpipe at the X Games at age thirteen and a gold medal a year later at age fourteen, then the youngest person to win a gold at the X Games.
- At Kim's first Winter Olympics in Pyeongchang, South Korea, she won the gold medal in the Women's Halfpipe finals.

Outcome: Kim was featured on the cover of *Sports Illustrated* following her Olympic gold medal win. Her appearance on a special edition of the Kellogg's Corn Flakes box set a new record for the fastest-selling cereal box in Kellogg's history. In 2018, Kim got a Shero Barbie in her likeness produced by Mattel and won three ESPY awards. She was admitted to Princeton University and is in the class of 2023.

Notes:

Athletic Genius
Passion To Paycheck Profiles

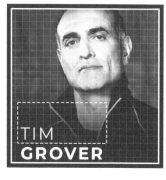

Tim **Grover**

Goal: Train professional athletes

Passion: Basketball

Talent: Exercise science

In Their Own Words: "To be the best, whether in sports or any business or any aspect of life, it's never enough to just get to the top; you have to stay there, and then you have to climb higher because there's always someone right behind you trying to catch up."

Passion to Paycheck: ├ ─ →

- Played Division I basketball at the University of Illinois, Chicago.

- Grover wrote his master's thesis on strength and conditioning for basketball players.

- Wrote fourteen individual letters to fourteen members of the Chicago Bulls offering his services (except Michael Jordan, thinking he was already too big to approach).

- After Michael Jordan became the only one interested, he gave Grover a thirty-day contract, and it turned into a fifteen-year partnership.

Outcome: Personal trainer for Michael Jordan, Charles Barkley, Kobe Bryant, Dwyane Wade, and more. He is the CEO of ATTACK ATHLETICS, which, according to its website, is "a company with a global staff of experts in cutting-edge physical therapy, sports medicine, nutrition, massage therapy, and vast resources in all areas of elite performance."

Notes:

_____

_____

Visual Genius

Passion To Paycheck Profiles

Individuals who are gifted
in the visual arts.

Visual Genius

Passion To Paycheck Profiles

Steve **Ditko**

Goal: Illustrate comics

Passion: Illustration

Talent: Drawing comic book characters

In Their Own Words: "If you have a certain point of view and reasons that you think are valid, then whether it's pro or anti, you can only and should only express those views you honestly hold."

Passion to Paycheck: ┝ ─ ➔

- Enlisted in the U.S. Army in 1945 and served in post WWII Germany, where he drew comics for an Army newspaper.

- Ditko enrolled in art school under the G.I. Bill, later earning a scholarship after learning that his idol, *Batman* artist Jerry Robinson, was teaching at the Cartoonists and Illustrators School (later the School of Visual Arts) in New York City.

- Started working at Atlas Comics the precursor to Marvel Comics in the 1950s.

- Created the drawing for *The Amazing Spiderman* in August 1962.

Outcome: Ditko also created the drawings for Doctor Octopus, Sandman, the Lizard, Green Goblin, and Dr. Strange and worked on the initial drawings for Iron Man and Hulk before leaving for DC Comics. Ditko was considered a reclusive genius, not comfortable with the limelight unlike Stan Lee. Although he died in relative obscurity, his mark on the comics and art world was praised by luminaries, including Neil Gaiman, Guillermo del Toro, and more when he passed away at age ninety.

Notes:

_____

_____

Virgil **Abloh**

Goal: Become a fashion designer

Passion: Designing high-end streetwear

Talent: Streetwear design

In Their Own Words: "When creativity melds together with global issues, I believe you can bring the world together."

Passion to Paycheck: ┣ - ➔

- Graduated from the University of Wisconsin-Madison with a Bachelor of Science in Civil Engineering.

- While studying for a Master's of Architecture, his interest in fashion was sparked, and he started designing t-shirts and writing about fashion and design on his blog, *The Brilliance.*

- Met Kanye West while working on his designs at a Chicago print shop and interned with him at Fendi.

- Founded Off-White, based in Milan, Italy, in 2013. Abloh described the brand as "the gray area between black and white as the color off-white" to investors and fashion critics.

Outcome: March 25, 2018, Abloh was named artistic director of Louis Vuitton's menswear ready-wear line, making him the first person of African descent to lead the brand's menswear line, while remaining the CEO of Off-White. He passed away in November 2021 at age 41.

Notes:

_____

_____

Visual Genius
Passion To Paycheck Profiles

Kaws (Brian Donnelly)

Goal: Become a pop artist

Passion: Graffiti

Talent: Fine art

In Their Own Words: "In my mind...art's purpose is to communicate and reach people. Whichever outlet that's being done through is the right one."

Passion to Paycheck: ├ ─ ➔

- Donnelly received a BFA in illustration from the School of Visual Arts in New York City in 1996.

- Worked as an animator by day painting backgrounds for series such as 101 *Dalmatians* and *Dari and Doug* while working as a graffiti artist by night.

- Began creating "subvertisements" after moving to New York City in the 1990s.

- In 1999, Kaws visited Japan after being approached by Bounty Hunter, the cult toy and streetwear brand. He would go on to create his first toy, "COMPANION."

Outcome: The first 500 COMPANION toys sold out almost immediately, and COMPANION became a recurring figure in Kaws' work. On April 1, 2019, at Sotheby's in Hong Kong, *The Kaws Album* (2005) sold for 115.9 million Hong Kong dollars, or about $14.7 million. In his work as a pop artist, Kaws collaborated with Nike, Uniqlo, and Hypebeast. Kaws is also a prolific art collector in his own right.

Notes:

Visual Genius

Passion To Paycheck Profiles

Sunny **Anderson**

Goal: Become a professional chef

Passion: Cooking

Talent: Culinary Arts

In Their Own Words: "I went broke, but I never lost my spirit. I was sleeping on a couch making money any way I could. I think you have to take a chance on yourself because nobody else will."

Passion to Paycheck: ⊢ - ➔

- Anderson joined the Air Force and worked as a radio broadcaster and journalist.

- After leaving the Air Force, she continued her travels as a radio DJ in many cities, culminating in her dream job at HOT 97 in New York City.

- In New York City, she began cooking for her friends in the entertainment business and turned her hobby and growing client list into a catering company.

- Made her first appearance on the Food Network's *Emeril Live!* in 2005.

Outcome: Anderson began hosting *How'd That Get on My Plate?* in July 2008. She also hosts the Food Network program *Cooking for Real* (beginning in April 2008) and served as co-host with Marc Istook of the Food Network program *Gotta Get It*. She published her New York Times bestselling cookbook, *Sunny's Kitchen: Easy Food for Real Life: A Cookbook* in 2013.

Notes:

_____

_____

_____

Social Genius

Passion To Paycheck Profiles

Individuals who are gifted with
the ability to lead and influence
others.

Oprah **Winfrey**

Goal: Become a media mogul

Passion: Storytelling, connecting with and inspiring others

Talent: Broadcast journalism and influencing people

In Their Own Words: "You don't become what you want, you become what you believe."

Passion to Paycheck: ⊢ - →

- Started public speaking as a young child reciting Bible verses in front of the congregation.

- Named the first black student body vice president and most popular girl at her high school.

- In 1972, at age 17, she won Miss Black Tennessee.

- Attended Tennessee State University and got her first on air television job in 1974.

- In 1985, the local *A.M. Chicago* television show was renamed *The Oprah Winfrey Show,* and she founded Harpo Studios the next year.

- Nominated for an Academy Award in 1986 for her role as Sofia in *The Color Purple.*

- After twenty-five seasons of the Oprah Winfrey Show, Oprah launched her own network, The Oprah Winfrey Network (OWN).

Outcome: Nicknamed "The Queen of All Media," Oprah became the first African American woman to become a billionaire with an estimated net worth of $2.6 billion. *The Oprah Winfrey Show* won sixteen Daytime Emmy Awards. She is also known as an actress, movie producer, media executive, author, and philanthropist.

Notes:

Social Genius

Passion To Paycheck Profiles

Gary **Vaynerchuk**

Goal: Build successful businesses that transcend culture and leave a legacy

Passion: The process of building businesses and inspiring others to prioritize happiness

Talent: Serial entrepreneurship

In Their Own Words: "The truth is that finding happiness in what you do every day is so imperative."

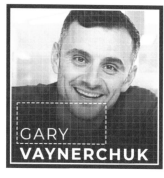

Passion to Paycheck: ┣ - →

- After graduating college in 1998, Gary took over daily operations of his father's liquor store, Shoppers Discount Liquors. He renamed it Wine Library, launched an e-commerce sales platform, and started his first YouTube show Wine Library TV in 2006. Gary grew his family's business from $3 million to $60 million in sales during a five-year period by leveraging the scalability of the internet.

- In 2008, Gary gave a keynote at Web 2.0 in New York City, which ultimately changed his career. That speech became the backbone of Gary's first book, *Crush It!* in 2009. Soon after, Gary began angel investing in notable companies including Facebook, Twitter, Tumblr, Uber, Snap, and Venmo.

- In 2009, Gary co-founded VaynerMedia, a digital marketing agency with his younger brother, A.J. Vaynerchuk. Today, VaynerMedia has over 1,000 employees servicing brands such as PepsiCo, GE, Johnson and Johnson, Chase AbInBev, and more. VaynerMedia has flourished as a best-in-class multi-media, strategy and creative agency with annual revenues surpassing $250 million.

Outcome: Gary is the chairman of VaynerX, a communication company that holds media properties and technology companies including Vayner Productions, Vayner Speakers, Vayner Commerce, Gallery Media Group, The Sasha Group, VNFT and more. In addition to running multiple businesses, Gary is a practitioner as a social media maven documenting his life as a CEO on his vlog Daily Vee. He has built an amazing personal brand with over 30 million followers across all platforms and his podcast *"The GaryVee Audio Experience"* ranks among the top globally. Gary is a five-time *New York Times* bestselling author and sought-after keynote speaker. He has an estimated net worth of $200 million.

Notes:

Social Genius

Passion To Paycheck Profiles

Casey **Neistat**

Goal: Filmmaking

Passion: Storytelling and making impactful video content

Talent: Creating innovative short films on social media platforms

In Their Own Words: "Without a goal, you can't score."

Passion to Paycheck: ┣ ─ ➤

- In 2001, Neistat and his brother worked with renowned artist Tom Sachs and made a series of films about Tom Sachs' sculptures and art installations.

- In 2003, Neistat gained international exposure for a three-minute film titled *iPod's Dirty Secret*. The film criticized Apple's lack of a battery replacement program.

- In 2008, HBO purchased an eight-episode television series, *The Neistat Brothers*, for just under $2 million.

Outcome: In 2016, Neistat received *GQ*'s "New Media Star" Man of the Year Award. In addition to his career in television and film, Neistat also directs and stars in television commercials, having worked with clients such as Samsung, Nike, Google, Finn Jewelry, J. Crew, and Mercedes-Benz. His YouTube channel currently has 12.4 million subscribers.

Notes:

_____

_____

_____

Charli **D'Amelio**

Goal: Social media influencer

Passion: Competitive Dancing

Talent: Choreography

In Their Own Words: "You just have to be authentic. You can't fake a smile. You have to do what you actually enjoy."

Passion to Paycheck: ┣ ─ ➔

- D'Amelio's career began on TikTok in the summer of 2019 after she uploaded dance videos to the platform's most popular songs.

- D'Amelio has over 100 million followers on TikTok and is listed as the platform's most powerful influencer.

- In January 2020, D'Amelio signed with talent agency UTA.

- Appeared in a Super Bowl commercial for Sabra Hummus and created the TikTok challenge, "J Lo Super Bowl Challenge," for Jennifer Lopez.

Outcome: According to a *Forbes* report published in August 2020, D'Amelio earned $4 million in 2019 from her numerous sponsorship deals and merchandise, making her the second highest-earning TikTok star. She and her family have also appeared in an eight-part Hulu series, *The D'Amelio Show*.

Notes:

_____

_____

_____

Tech Genius

Passion To Paycheck Profiles

Individuals who are gifted with the ability to develop problem-solving software, hardware, and gaming solutions.

MORGAN DEBAUN

MARK ZUCKERBERG

TYLER "NINJA" BLEVINS

TRISTAN WALKER

Tech Genius
Passion To Paycheck Profiles

Morgan **Debaun**

Goal: Create media platforms that celebrate and advance black culture

Passion: Business, technology, and positive representation of black culture in the media

Talent: Entrepreneurship and business management

In Their Own Words: "Execution and failure is a part of the process. You have to accept that."

Passion to Paycheck: ⊢ - →

- DeBaun graduated from Washington University in St. Louis with a major in political science and minors in entrepreneurship and education.

- In 2012, she headed to Silicon Valley to work at Intuit with a focus on product management and business development.

- In 2014, she launched Blavity (Black + Gravity), the largest media startup and lifestyle brand for black millennials, with her co-founders (Aaron Samuels, Jonathan Jackson, and Jeff Nelson). Under her leadership, Blavity has successfully acquired multiple companies and raised millions in venture funding.

Outcome: Since launching Blavity, Inc. in 2014, the media brand has grown to reach 100 million monthly reader/viewership targeting black millennials globally. Morgan has led the company to successfully acquire and/or build their brand portfolio to include Blavity News, AfroTech, Travel Noire, Shadow and Act, 21Ninety, and Lunchtable. Morgan is one of a few African American female founders to raise more than $1 million in venture capital and to date has raised over $12 million from top Silicon Valley venture firms. Additionally, she is a sought-after speaker, business advisor and listed by Forbes as one of the most influential women in technology.

Notes:

Tech Genius
Passion To Paycheck Profiles

Mark **Zuckerberg**

Goal: Build the world's largest social network

Passion: Developing software

Talent: Software engineering and writing code

In Their Own Words: "Find that thing you are super passionate about."

Passion to Paycheck: ⊢ - ➔

- Zuckerberg took a graduate course in programming at Mercy College while still in high school.

- Enrolled at Harvard University in 2002 and started Facemash his sophomore year.

- After Facemash was pulled down, Zuckerberg created thefacebook.com, which later became facebook.com.

- Zuckerberg dropped out of Harvard his sophomore year. As the site's popularity expanded, it branched off to include students at other schools before taking off as the leading social network.

Outcome: Facebook filed its IPO with the Securities and Exchange Commission on February 1, 2012. At that time, it was the largest technology IPO in US history. As of fall 2021, the company boasted 2.89 billion active monthly users and changed its parent company's name to Meta as it ushers in Web 3.0 metaverse business initiatives. Zuckerberg, himself, is listed as being worth $100 billion, and Facebook is valued at $930 billion.

Notes:

_____

_____

Tyler **"Ninja" Blevins**

Goal: Become a professional gamer

Passion: Playing video games

Talent: Gaming

In Their Own Words: "People need to be true to themselves, and if entertaining and content-creating is something that does not come naturally and is really difficult, they should find something they are passionate about and love and do that instead."

Passion to Paycheck: ⊢ - →

- Blevins began playing *Halo 3* professionally in 2009 at age ten and became a streamer in 2011.

- Won the *PUBG* Gamescom Invitational Squads classification in August 2017.

- According to the *Chicago Tribune*, on March 14, 2018, Blevins set the Twitch record for a single individual stream when more than 600,000 concurrent viewers tuned in to watch him play Fortnite with Drake, Travis Scott, and Pittsburgh Steelers wide receiver, Juju Smith-Schuster.

- Ninja has more than seventeen million followers on Twitch, more than fourteen million followers on Instagram, and more than twenty-four million subscribers on YouTube.

Outcome: Ninja said his goal is to have gaming respected and viewed as a career possibility in the same way as professional football, basketball, and baseball. As of 2020, Blevins is estimated to make $20 million annually.

Notes:

_____

_____

Tech Genius

Passion To Paycheck Profiles

Tristan **Walker**

Goal: Found multicultural technology and consumer businesses

Passion: Creating consumer products that leverage technology and service minority communities.

Talent: Business management and entrepreneurship

In Their Own Words: "The best ideas are brewed out of authenticity."

Passion to Paycheck: ┣ ─ ➔

- Unhappy on Wall Street, Walker applied to Stanford Business School with an eye on working in Silicon Valley.

- Interned at Twitter and the Boston Consulting Group while studying for his MBA.

- Turned down a permanent position at another company and started emailing Dennis Crowley, co-founder and CEO of Foursquare, who eventually hired him.

- After leaving Foursquare, Walker took a position as entrepreneur-in-residence at Andreesseen Horowitz.

- After going through a series of ideas, Walker eventually landed on Walker & Co. to address the health and beauty needs of minorities.

Outcome: Walker & Co. launched with its first product, Bevel, a single-blade razor system, in 2014. Founding Walker & Co. in spring 2013, he raised $6.9 million in seed funding. The company raised a second funding round in 2015, this time amounting to $25 million from top venture capitalists and celebrity investors. They also announced a partnership with Target to carry Bevel in select stores and on Target.com. According to Fast Company, in 2018, Procter & Gamble, the consumer packaged goods conglomerate known for such household staples as Tide and Old Spice, acquired Walker & Company Brands.

Notes:

Number Genius
Passion To Paycheck Profiles

Individuals who are gifted in
mathematics, science, logic,
and reasoning.

Number Genius

Passion To Paycheck Profiles

Robert **F. Smith**

Goal: Become a successful private equity manager and venture capitalist

Passion: Investing in technology and software companies

Talent: Business management, finance, and engineering

In Their Own Words: "Have the vision of what you want to become, but you have to put consistent action behind the vision in order for that to manifest."

Passion to Paycheck: ┝ ─ ➤

- Smith graduated from Cornell University with a degree in chemical engineering and worked at Kraft Foods and Goodyear Tire before getting his MBA at Columbia University with concentrations in finance and marketing, according to his company website, www.vistaequitypartners.com.

- Smith then worked at Goldman Sachs in New York City and Silicon Valley in mergers and acquisitions.

- In 2000, Mr. Smith co-founded Vista Equity Partner with Brian Sheth, focusing on investing in the technology, software, and data sectors.

Outcome: As of 2019, Vista Equity Partners had closed more than $46 billion of funding. Smith counts his net worth as $7 billion. Smith is also a committed philanthropist, having overseen donations to Cornell University, the National Park Foundation, and the United Negro College Fund as a part of Fund II Fund, an organization that also bought Martin Luther King Jr.'s home for preservation in 2019. In 2015, Smith sponsored the college education of all returned Boko Haram girls. Smith gained major press in 2019 for pledging to pay off $34 million in student debt for graduating Morehouse College students.

Notes:

Number Genius

Passion To Paycheck Profiles

Warren **Buffet**

Goal: Become one of the world's greatest investors

Passion: Investing

Talent: Mathematics and business management

In Their Own Words: "Without passion, you don't have energy, without energy you have nothing."

Passion to Paycheck: ⊢ - ➔

- Buffett bought his first stock at age eleven at $38 which quickly dropped to $27, scaring a young Buffett who sold it at $40. When it later went up to $200, he learned his investing mantra—patience is a virtue.

- Entered the Wharton School of Business at the University of Pennsylvania in 1947 before transferring to and graduating from the University of Nebraska at nineteen. He went on to graduate from Columbia Business School.

- In 1956, Buffett created Buffett Partnership, Ltd. and eventually acquired a textile manufacturing firm called Berkshire Hathaway. Berkshire Hathaway now owns Fruit of the Loom, Geico, Duracell, and many other companies.

- Buffett became a billionaire when Berkshire Hathaway began selling class A shares on May 29, 1990.

Outcome: Buffett is considered one of the most successful investors in the world and has a net worth of $110.5 billion as of January 2022, making him the world's seventh-wealthiest person. He has pledged to give away 99 percent of his wealth.

Notes:

Katherine **Johnson**

Goal: Become a mathematician

Passion: Data analysis and calculating spacecraft flight patterns

Talent: Mathematics and electronic computation

In Their Own Words: "Like what you do, and then you will do your best. . . I loved going to work every day."

Passion to Paycheck: ├ ─ →

- At age eighteen, Johnson enrolled in the HBCU West Virginia State College.

- In 1939, she was selected to be among the first three black students to integrate the graduate school of West Virginia University.

- In 1952, Johnson joined the all-black West Area Computing section at the National Advisory Committee for Aeronautics' (NACA's) Langley Laboratory (now known as Langley Research Center) in Virginia.

- Earned her first claim to fame by working on the computations for John Glenn's 1962 orbital mission.

Outcome: Johnson also worked on the space shuttle and the Earth Resources Technology Satellite (ERTS, later renamed Landsat) and authored or coauthored twenty-six research reports. She retired in 1986 after thirty-three years at Langley. Her life story, along with two of her NASA coworkers, inspired the hit book and film *Hidden Figures*. In 2015, at age ninety-seven, Johnson received a Presidential Medal of Freedom, the highest civilian honor, from President Barack Obama.

Notes:

Number Genius
Passion To Paycheck Profiles

Neil Degrasse **Tyson**

Goal: Become an astrophysicist

Passion: Science and astronomy

Talent: Popular science education

In Their Own Words: "Passion is what gets you through the hardest times that might . . . make you give up."

Passion to Paycheck: ⊢ ‑ →

- Graduated from Harvard with a degree in physics and earned a PhD in astrophysics from Columbia.

- Went to work at Hayden Planetarium and in 2006 began hosting *NOVA ScienceNow*.

- In 2009, Tyson started StarTalk, first a radio show, now a podcast, that explores science with comedic co-hosts. It led to the launch of his TV show, *StarTalk*.

- In 2014, Tyson hosted a thirteen-episode television series entitled *Cosmos: A Space-Time Odyssey*, a reboot of the classic science documentary, *Cosmos*.

Outcome: Tyson has authored over a dozen books and received twenty honorary doctorates. He has won numerous awards, including a Grammy for a spoken word album and a YouTube Gold Play Button Creator Award. Tyson continues to work as the Director of the Hayden Planetarium, a position he's held since 1996.

Notes:

Eco Genius

Passion To Paycheck Profiles

Individuals who are gifted with the love and appreciation for the Earth, animals, and all parts of nature.

JADEN **SMITH**

AL **GORE**

BLAKE **MYCOSKIE**

MATT **DAMON**

Eco Genius

Passion To Paycheck Profiles

Jaden **Smith**

Goal: Reduce the use of plastic and provide clean water to underserved communities

Passion: Sustainability and helping others

Talent: Mobilizing and influencing others to create sustainable change

In Their Own Words: "My whole goal is to heal the entire planet. . . I want to heal the whole world like a superhero would do."

Passion to Paycheck: ┠ – ➜

- At ten years old, Jaden Smith launched the idea for JUST after seeing plastic trash floating around him while surfing.

- In high school, Smith learned about the Great Pacific Garbage Patch, floating islands of garbage and plastic debris, and insisted his family do something about it.

- In 2015, at age seventeen, with the help of his parents, Will and Jada Smith, Jaden founded JUST Water selling responsibly sourced water from upstate New York in a carton made of 82 percent renewable resources.

- In 2019, partnered with a Flint, Michigan church to deploy a mobile lead filtration system after the Flint Water Crisis of 2014.

Outcome: JUST is currently in fifteen thousand retail locations in North America and twenty-one thousand stores in Japan. JUST water has a $100 million valuation and is a certified B Corp, maintaining and upholding rigorous standards of social and environmental performance. JUST announced in August 2020 that the company will boost capacity to 100 million boxes a year. Jaden's New Balance Vision Racer sneakers are also partially made of recycled materials.

Notes:

Eco Genius
Passion To Paycheck Profiles

Al **Gore**

Goal: Promote the seriousness of global climate change

Passion: Educating the public on climate change problems and solutions

Talent: Using media and his influence to promote environmental causes

In Their Own Words: "We must protect and preserve our planet for future generations. Once we find the courage to change, we can create a world that our children and grandchildren can safely inhabit."

Passion to Paycheck: ┝ ━ ➤

- At twenty-eight, after joining the United States House of Representatives, Gore held the first congressional hearings on climate change in 1976.

- As Bill Clinton's vice president, Gore launched the GLOBE program, a science education program for primary and secondary school students, on Earth Day in 1994.

- In the late 1990s, Gore strongly pushed for the passage of the Kyoto Protocol, which called for reduction in greenhouse gas emissions.

- As a private citizen, Gore devoted himself to climate change issues through promoting green investment strategies, films, and public relations campaigns.

Outcome: Gore's documentary, *An Inconvenient Truth*, won two Oscars in 2006. In 2007, Gore was awarded the Nobel Peace Prize, along with the Intergovernmental Panel on Climate Change, for his work on environmental matters.

Notes:

Eco Genius

Passion To Paycheck Profiles

Blake **Mycoskie**

Goal: Create a business to improve lives and promote corporate responsibility and conscious consumerism

Passion: Conscious entrepreneurship

Talent: Innovating and problem solving around sustainable business practices

In Their Own Words: "Anyone can make a difference, so you don't have to have it be some huge global campaign. You can start small and that's just as important."

Passion to Paycheck: ┣ - →

- Before TOMS, Mycoskie started five businesses. His first was a successful campus laundry service.

- The idea for a for-profit business with a core charitable component came from a trip to Argentina in 2006, where Mycoskie saw the hardships faced by children without shoes.

- Mycoskie, who got used to wearing the national shoe—the *alpargata*, a soft, casual canvas shoe worn by almost everyone in Argentina—thought the shoe could become popular in the United States.

- Mycoksie decided for every pair of the Toms shoes sold, he would give a new pair of shoes to a child in need.

Outcome: TOMS has expanded its line beyond shoes to include sunglasses and other accessories. Since its launch in 2006, TOMS has partnered with countless organizations such as UNICEF, Save the Children, Partners in Health, the Red Cross, Everytown, Faith in Action, March for Our Lives, and others. On August 20, 2014, Bain Capital acquired 50 percent of TOMS. Reuters reported that the transaction valued the company at $625 million. According to the TOMS Impact Report, it's estimated that as of late 2019, TOMS has donated more than 96.5 million pairs of shoes to those in need.

Notes:

Eco Genius

Passion To Paycheck Profiles

Matt **Damon**

Goal: Help solve the global water crisis

Passion: Raising awareness about safe water initiatives in Africa

Talent: Acting, philanthropy and using his influence for social change

In Their Own Words: "You will never solve poverty without solving water and sanitation."

Passion to Paycheck: ⊢ - ➤

- After filming a movie in Zambia, Damon spent time with families who lacked access to clean water and indoor plumbing.

- To raise awareness about clean water initiatives on the continent, Damon founded H2O Africa Foundation in 2006.

- In 2008, during an annual Clinton Global Initiative meeting in New York, Damon met Gary White, an engineer from Kansas City who had gained an international reputation as a water and sanitation expert.

- White and Damon then partnered together and merged H2O Africa and Water Partners International to create Water.org in 2009.

Outcome: Water.org is now operating in thirteen countries and has provided thirty million people with safe water or sanitation.

Notes:

Word Genius

Passion To Paycheck Profiles

Individuals who are gifted with the ability to communicate through the written word.

Word Genius
Passion To Paycheck Profiles

J.K. **Rowling**

Goal: Become a published author

Passion: Literature and storytelling

Talent: Writing fiction for children and adults

In Their Own Words: "As soon as I knew what writers were, I wanted to be one. I've got the perfect temperament for a writer; perfectly happy alone in a room, making things up."

Passion to Paycheck: ┣ - ➔

- According to her website, J.K. wrote her first book at the age of six—a story about a rabbit called *Rabbit*.

- Also, according to the author, at just eleven, she wrote her first novel—about seven cursed diamonds and the people who owned them.

- While sitting on a train in London, Rowling conceived the idea for the Harry Potter series.

- J.K. worked on her first Harry Potter book while on public assistance, and the first Harry Potter book was published in 1997.

Outcome: Harry Potter is now a global brand featuring movies, merchandise, and books worth an estimated $15 billion. The series has been translated into sixty-five languages. J.K. also published a mystery series for adults, under a pseudonym Robert Galbraith. J.K. is reportedly the first author to reach a $1 billion net worth, according to *Forbes*.

Notes:

Ryan **Coogler**

Goal: Write and direct culturally relevant movies

Passion: Multicultural filmmaking and storytelling

Talent: Screenwriting and directing

In Their Own Words: "I grew up very much into pop culture, very into comic books, so [working with Marvel is] something that is just as personal to me as the last couple of films [*Fruitvale Station* + *Creed*] I was able to make. I feel really fortunate to be able to work on something I'm this passionate about again."

Passion to Paycheck: ⊢ - →

- Encouraged to take up screenwriting by a creative writing professor at St. Mary's College of California, where he attended on a football scholarship.

- Following graduation, Coogler was accepted into the highly competitive three-year master's program at the USC School of Cinematic Arts.

- At the USC School of Cinematic Arts, Coogler directed four short films, garnering three award nominations.

- *Fruitvale Station*, his first feature-length film, starred Michael B. Jordan and won the top Audience Award and Grand Jury Prize at the 2013 Sundance Film Festival.

Outcome: In 2013, MGM sought Coogler to direct *Creed*, a spin-off sequel of the *Rocky* films. Coogler co-wrote the film with Aaron Covington. Coogler then went on to co-write and direct *Black Panther*. *Black Panther* grossed the fifth largest opening weekend box-office of all time and ended up grossing $1.29 billion at the box office worldwide. Coogler has been signed up to write and direct *Black Panther 2* and served as a producer on *Space Jam: A New Legacy* starring Lebron James.

Notes:

Stan **Lee**

Goal: Become a professional writer

Passion: Comic books and storytelling

Talent: Writing and creating comic book characters

In Their Own Words: "If you are interested in what you do, that keeps you going."

Passion to Paycheck: ├ ─ ➔

- Lee wrote obituaries for the local paper and National Tuberculosis Center when he was a teenager.
- Got hired as an assistant at Timely Comics in 1939, which became Marvel Comics in 1960s.
- Got his first credits writing text filler for "Captain America Foils the Traitor's Revenge" in *Captain America Comics* #3.
- Created Spider-Man with artist Steve Ditko in 1962.
- Retired from writing monthly comics in 1972 to become publisher of Marvel. His final issue of *The Amazing Spider-Man* was #110 (July 1972), and his last *Fantastic Four* was #125 (August 1972).

Outcome: Began developing Marvel's TV properties in 1981 and served as an executive producer for and made cameo appearances in many Marvel TV shows and films. Stan Lee had an estimated net worth of $50 million at the time of his death. As of September 2021, The Marvel characters created by Lee have made over $20 billion at the box office according to *Forbes*.

Notes:

Word Genius
Passion To Paycheck Profiles

Lena **Waithe**

Goal: Write and produce multicultural television shows and movies

Passion: Multicultural writing and storytelling

Talent: Creating dynamic screenplays and teleplays

In Their Own Words: "You can talk all day long, but if you don't do something, it's a waste."

Passion to Paycheck: ┝ - →

- Graduated from Columbia College Chicago with a degree in Cinema and Television Arts.

- Got her first job as an assistant to the executive producer of the television show *Girlfriends*.

- Became a writer on the TV series *Bones* and executive produced the film *Dear White People*.

- In 2017, became the first black American woman to win an Emmy for Outstanding Writing for a Comedy Series for her work on *Master of None*.

Outcome: Waithe founded her own production company, Hillman Grad Productions, and became the showrunner and creator for the Showtime series called *The Chi. Out Magazine* named Waithe the Out 100: Artist of the Year in November 2017. Waithe wrote and produced the road trip/crime film *Queen & Slim* starring Jodie Turner-Smith and Daniel Kaluuya, directed by Melina Matsoukas. It was released on November 27, 2019, by Universal Pictures.

Notes:

_____

_____

_____

Spiritual Genius

Passion To Paycheck Profiles

Individuals who are gifted with
a higher calling beyond the
material world.

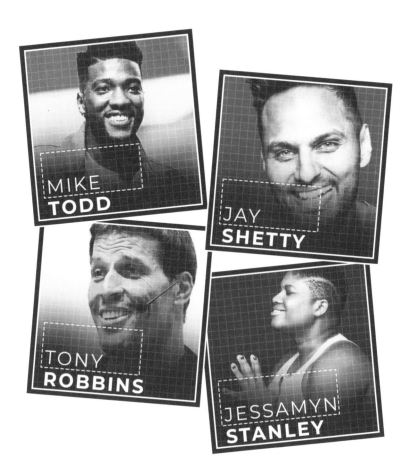

Spiritual Genius
Passion To Paycheck Profiles

Michael **Todd**

Goal: Become an inspirational pastor

Passion: Delivering non-traditional and timeless motivational sermons

Talent: Presenting religion and relationship counseling in a modern way

In Their Own Words: "I've noticed that one of the key issues that hinders people from reaching their relationship goals is the fact that they don't know how to aim."

Passion to Paycheck: ⊢ - →

- Todd grew up as a church musician focusing on drums and percussion.

- Started So FLY (Sold Out Free Life Youth) youth and young adults ministry.

- In 2015, at age twenty-eight, Michael along with his wife, Natalie, became lead pastors of Transformation Church in Tulsa, Oklahoma.

- Their sermon series, *Relationship Goals*, went viral, reaching millions of people and gaining six million views in two years.

Outcome: Todd's energetic, modern approach to Christianity and viral videos led to him writing two *New York Times* bestsellers, *Relationship Goals and Crazy Faith*. Michael and his wife are in demand speakers both in the United States and internationally. Their ministry reaches 5,000 people each week in person and 20,000 people online.

Notes:

_____

_____

_____

_____

Spiritual Genius

Passion To Paycheck Profiles

Jay **Shetty**

Goal: Helping others discover their purpose and live fulfilled lives

Passion: Inspiring people to find purpose in life

Talent: Teaching mindfulness and self-growth

In Their Own Words: "It's important to figure out who you're not, in order to figure out who you are."

Passion to Paycheck: ┣ ─ ➔

- During business school, Shetty trained in India to be a monk.

- At age twenty-six, Shetty was $25,000 in debt and living with his parents, directionless and depressed.

- Worked as a corporate digital strategist for Accenture but left seeking a higher purpose.

- Applied his studies as a monk to stress management and workplace productivity to create viral videos.

Outcome: Shetty was eventually hired by the *Huffington Post* to create videos on relationships, wellness, mental health, and purpose. Shetty's podcast, *On Purpose*, reached fifty-two million downloads in his first year and became the number-one health podcast in the world, according to *Forbes*. Shetty's book, *Think Like a Monk*, was a *New York Times* bestseller, and Shetty is now a full-time purpose coach.

Notes:

_____

_____

_____

_____

Spiritual Genius

Passion To Paycheck Profiles

Tony **Robbins**

Goal: Become a global thought leader and lifestyle success coach

Passion: Helping individuals define success and achieve it

Talent: Inspiring and motivating people to find their greatness

In Their Own Words: "Without passion, an individual gets caught in the trap of making a living instead of designing a life."

Passion to Paycheck: ⊢ - →

- Left home at seventeen and began promoting self-help seminars for motivational speaker and author Jim Rohn.

- In 1988, Robbins released his first infomercial for his self-help program, Personal Power, and in 1997, Robbins launched the Leadership Academy seminar.

- Robbins founded the Robbins-Madanes Training Center in 2002 with Cloe Madanes.

- Robbins has written six internationally bestselling books, including the recent New York Times financial bestsellers, MONEY: Master the Game and UNSHAKEABLE.

Outcome: Mr. Robbins is the chairman of a holding company composed of more than seventy privately held businesses with combined sales exceeding $6 billion annually. He has worked with four US presidents, top entertainers—including Aerosmith, Green Day, Usher, and Pitbull—and athletes and sports teams—including tennis world champion Serena Williams and the NBA's world champion Golden State Warriors. Robbins is also an active philanthropist and is considered a major thought leader on self-improvement.

Notes:

Spiritual Genius

Passion To Paycheck Profiles

Jessamyn **Stanley**

Goal: Promote body positivity and self-love

Passion: Yoga, mindfulness, and celebrating body positivity in all people

Talent: Vinyasa flow yoga and influencing others

In Their Own Words: "Yoga has given me the space to understand that every part of me is necessary. Everything is exactly as it needs to be. And what needs to be silenced are the voices that make me feel otherwise."

Passion to Paycheck: ⊢ - →

- Tried yoga first as a sixteen-year-old and hated it.

- Committed to yoga in her twenties as a way of dealing with depression and to develop a spiritual connection.

- Gained attention in 2012 after posting images of herself on Instagram doing yoga poses.

- Completed 230-hour teacher training program at Asheville Yoga Center in North Carolina.

Outcome: Stanley's status as a social media influencer has led her to partner with many brands, including Lane Bryant, Motrin, and Kotex Fitness. She has appeared on the covers of *Cosmopolitan* and *Yoga Journal* and is the author of *Every Body Yoga* and *Yoke: My Yoga of Self-Acceptance.*

Notes:

_____

_____

_____

_____

_____

Genius Factor Mapping
Passion To Paycheck
Summary Questions

- My name is

_____

- I am passionate about

_____

_____

- My God-given talents are

_____

_____

- My genius factor is

_____

_____

- The industry and job/profession that best align with my genius factor(s) are

_____

_____

- I can get started in this industry by doing

_____

_____

- I can get valuable experience by doing

_____

_____

- The college major that best corresponds with the industry I wish to pursue is

_____

_____

- After reviewing all relevant passion to paycheck profiles, what similar steps did each individual take to achieve success?

_____

_____

- Research: What internships, apprenticeship and/or jobs best correspond to my industry of choice?

_____

_____

- Research: How can I identify and find mentors within my industry of choice?

_____

_____

 "Success is a habit and the secret to your future is hidden in your daily routine."

Genius Factor Activation:
The Playbook

In the section, you will develop a customized playbook for activating your genius factor in day-to-day life. This passion to paycheck blueprint is the culmination of the work you have done in discovering and mapping your genius factor. This document will help you create clearly defined strategies to accelerate your career pathway so work and play are one. There are five major plays to the genius factor playbook, and you must complete all of them. This is a critically important exercise, so take your time and be thoughtful with your answers. This is your life and your playbook, and it's totally on you to execute and make your passion your paycheck.

PLAY #1

Genius Factor Discovery x Mapping Summary

This is the summary of the work completed in the genius factor discovery and mapping sections. It is designed to be a quick reference for the factors that have influenced your genius.

Please fill out this section and use it as a self-check to keep yourself honest as you work towards your goals.

Genius Factor

Playbook Discover x Mapping Summary

Genius Factor:

I'm a ...

-

-

Passion:

I'm PASSIONATE about ...

-

-

-

Talents:

My GOD given TALENTS are ...

-

-

-

Professions/Jobs:

In alignment with my GENIUS are ...

-

-

-

PLAY #2

Dreams x Goals

Writing down your dreams and goals will significantly increase your ability to accomplish them.

This section will help you outline short-term and long-term dreams/goals and make sure to use the S.M.A.R.T goals checklist as you complete this portion of your playbook.

Genius Factor

Dreams x Goals

DREAMS

Short-Term (1 - 5 years)

1.

2.

3.

4.

5.

6.

Long-Term (6 - 15 years)

1.

2.

3.

4.

5.

6.

GOALS

Short-Term (1 - 5 years)

1.

2.

3.

4.

5.

6.

Long-Term (6 - 15 years)

1.

2.

3.

4.

5.

6.

S.M.A.R.T GOALS CHECKLIST:

- Specific – Exactly what you want
- Measurable – Metrics for evaluating progress
- Achievable – Must be reasonable
- Relevant – Align with your passion and genius factor
- Timely – Timeframe/target completion date

PLAY #3

G.O.S.T Strategic Thinking Framework

Goals, Objectives, Strategies, Tactics (G.O.S.T) is a framework to help you think strategically about how to achieve your goals

Please see the example I've created that illustrates how I used the G.O.S.T method to achieve one of my personal goals and use it as a primer to fill out the section for yourself.

G.O.S.T
Strategic Thinking Framework

Goals: These are high level descriptors of the desired outcomes you wish to create. (qualitative - traits & charactersitics)

* _____

* _____

* _____

Objectives: Specific outcomes that define your goals (quantitative - measured using numbers)

* _____

* _____

* _____

Strategies: Plan outlining path you will follow to achieve objectives that directly map to your goals

* _____

* _____

* _____

Tactics: Series of specific smaller tasks that are the building blocks of your strategies

* _____

* _____

* _____

EXAMPLE:
The Torrance Hampton Brand

Goals:

Torrance Hampton is the global thought leader on "Making Your Passion Your Paycheck," and helping all individuals unlock Passion, Genius Factor & Happiness.

Objectives:

Increase national brand profile via book, public speaking & online course sales by 300% over the next 24 months.

Strategies:

Write "Genius Factor" book and develop scalable online course targeting high school & college students (Gen Z + Gen Y), as well as adults (Gen X) who feel lost and struggling to find direction in life.

Tactics:

Launch book and online course with renown publicist via national book signing and speaking tour at high schools, colleges and professional conferences both domestic & international.

PLAY #4

Internships|Apprenticeships|Jobs x Mentorship

Internships, apprenticeships, and jobs are extremely important to gain experience in your field of choice. Start researching the opportunities that exist and prioritize below based on application deadlines.

This section will also help with weekly accountability to make sure you are organized and staying ahead of all opportunities.

Internships|Apprenticeships|Jobs

There are three ways to get real world experiences: internships, apprenticeships, or jobs. Internships are valuable because they provide real-world experience and access to individuals in the professions in which you are interested. Apprenticeships are slightly different because they provide targeted job experience with the possibility of full-time employment. This builds your network and allows you to get first-hand experiences working with potentially influential individuals and possible mentors. Jobs do the same while paying you to gain valuable experience. Regardless of the path you choose, the bottom line to all of this is you must jump in and get to work!

Mentorship

I define a mentor as someone who is invested in your success. A mentor is also someone who has expert knowledge in specific careers that interest you. For example, one of my most impactful mentors was the late Jack Hartmann—a brilliant director and cinematographer. I had the pleasure of working with Jack on multiple projects, and he taught me the art of storytelling. I started G|FACTOR FILMS as a direct result of his mentorship and wisdom. He shared priceless insights from his years of filmmaking experience, and it gave me the confidence to pursue my dream as a filmmaker and director. Mentors are critically important to activate your genius factor. It's important that you find the right mentor as soon as possible because they will significantly shorten your learning curve. The right mentors are magical, so choose wisely!

Genius Factor

Internships x Apprenticeships x Jobs x Mentorship

Internships | Apprenticeships | Jobs
Identify Opportunities

1. _____

2. _____

3. _____

4. _____

5. _____

6. _____

Mentors
Identify Individuals

1. _____

2. _____

3. _____

4. _____

5. _____

6. _____

Weekly Accountability Report

1. _____

2. _____

3. _____

4. _____

5. _____

6. _____

Weekly Accountability Report

1. _____

2. _____

3. _____

4. _____

5. _____

6. _____

Notes: _____

_____

_____

PLAY #5
Affirmations x Mindfulness

Affirmations and mindfulness are habits that many highly successful individuals practice daily. These habits map to mastering the law of attraction—*like attracts like*. What you think about you bring about. Your words and thoughts are powerful, so it's very important to feed your conscious and subconscious mind with positive phrases.

Please fill out this portion of your playbook and use it as a guide to develop these success habits as part of your daily routine.

Affirmations x Mindfulness

Affirmations are positive statements that fuel the law of attraction and help you overcome self-sabotage and negative thoughts. Mindfulness is the practice of focusing your awareness on the present moment and is often associated with meditation. Both are part of my daily routine and have positively impacted my ability to manifest and achieve my goals faster.

As an example, I practice mindfulness daily through prayer/meditation, and one of my favorite daily affirmations is: There is nothing I cannot do. There is nothing I cannot be. There is nothing I cannot have. Let the Genius within me now be released!

Genius Factor

Affirmations x Mindfulness

AFFIRMATIONS
Daily Routine:

1. _____
2. _____
3. _____
4. _____
5. _____
6. _____

Weekly Accountability Report

1. _____
2. _____
3. _____
4. _____
5. _____
6. _____

MINDFULLNESS
Daily Routine:

1. _____
2. _____
3. _____
4. _____
5. _____
6. _____

Weekly Accountability Report

1. _____
2. _____
3. _____
4. _____
5. _____
6. _____

Torrance Hampton
Daily Affirmation:

There is nothing I cannot do.
There is nothing I cannot be.
There is nothing I cannot have.
Let the Genius within me
now be released!

THE LAW OF ATTRACTION

- Like attracts like! What you think about, you bring about.

- Your thoughts become things, so it's critically important to feed your conscious and subconscious mind on a daily basis with positive words and thoughts!

Parting Thoughts

As I think about my journey to discovering my genius factor, all the ups and downs, all the frustrating moments and massive failures, I'm left asking myself one question: Do I have any regrets? My response: I only have one regret. I wish I had known how to apply the steps to discover my genius factor much earlier in life. And that, my friends, is the ultimate teachable moment from this book. Don't wait on pursuing the life you want, the life that's filled with joy and happiness. Have a sense of urgency to go make it happen and have the courage to chase your dreams. Additionally, you must turn down the noise that's in your head and stop listening to others' opinions on what you should be doing. Trust me, they don't know what's best for you, but you do! Tap into your self-awareness and start listening to the inner voice that's whispering in your head. That's the voice you should trust—the one that is speaking directly to your passion, the thing that sets your soul on fire, the thing that everyone says is crazy. Remember this: it's only crazy until you do it, then they will say you're a genius. And you know what? They're one hundred percent correct!

Thank you for taking time to read this book. I'm truly humbled by the gesture. I pray this book is a catalyst for sustainable happiness in your life. A life where work and play are one, and a life where you're making your passion your paycheck.

 When your heart decides the destination, your mind will design the playbook to get there.

Acknowledgements

The fact that I wrote this book is absolutely insane to me. As a kid, I didn't like reading and struggled to pay attention and comprehend anything I read. I remember thinking I would never write a book, and yet, here we are, and I am ecstatic about it. This book marks a major milestone in my life, especially since I first started writing it in 2016, but more importantly, it's me keeping a promise to myself and my mom. There are so many people who deserve acknowledgement in this book, and I apologize in advance if your name is not mentioned. I want to thank everyone who had an impact on me and helped shape my life. I'm grateful!

First, I want to acknowledge my family: my wife, Dr. Alena C. Hampton, and my two amazing children, London (aka L-Money) and Torrance, II (aka T2). I'm grateful for your unwavering love and support, and I thank God every day for allowing me to have you in my life! I also want to acknowledge the inspiration for this book, my mom, Margie Hampton; my dad, Tommy Hampton; my stepmother, Gladys Hampton; my brother, Dr. Chadwick Hampton (and his family: Thierry, Milan); and my sister, Mia Dickerson (and her family: Brandon, Christian, Faith). I want to give a special shout out to my two favorite uncles, Dr. Randall Little and Dr. Chester Little. You both had such a significant and priceless impact on my childhood, and I want to say thank you and I love you both! Additionally, I want to give a special thank you to my co-author Christina Morgan. I'm extremely grateful for your time on this project and amazing talent as an author. Finally, I want to acknowledge all my extended family and close friends. I love you guys tremendously, and I'm grateful for all your love and support through the years.

Second, I want to thank all the individuals (friends and family) who have mentored, inspired, and shaped me throughout my life. This list is not in any particular order, but the people listed have all had profound impacts on my life. T.C. Little (grandfather), Ray Helen Little (grandmother), Willie Hampton (grandfather), Bessie Harmon Hampton (grandmother), Dr. Randall Little, Dr. Chester Little, Alex & Erin Little, Phil Little, Ruth Little, Ron and Connie Young, Hubert and Satwant Bell, Alonzo and Sandy Webb, Robert and Shelly Boswell, Michael Hampton, Nicholas "Dad" Hampton, Bessie Hampton, Ronald Betton, Marie

Torrance Hampton

Betton, Bishop Timothy Clark, Pastor Lance Watson, Pastor Norman Tate, Gerald & Angie Claiborne, Leah Claiborne, Tiffany Claiborne, Reverend Anthony and Brenda McMichael, Andrea McMichael, William "Coco" McMichael, Joy Allen, Ada Evans, Justin Byrd, Garvin Byrd, Al Byrd, Sr, Al Byrd, Jr, Adiclere Evans, Monique McCloud-Manley, Danielle Rose, Dr. Kelly Bolden, Andrea Hence-Evans, Robert Rumley, Kenneth Saffold, Julian Montgomery, Raaquim Knight, Damon Boswell, Torarie Durden, Henry Stewart, William Cole aka Gym Jonez, Alvin "Mr. D." Dickenson, Justin Gray, Andrea Gray, Bill Gray, Andrew Gray, Ruston Spurlock, Ed Tapscott, Janice Thomas, Christopher Harrison, Ted Jeffries, Kia Lowe, Carl & Sandy Lowe, Robert Collins, Sekou Murray, Star Dillard, Capo The Kid, Dionne Lewis Burkett, Scooby "King of Keno" Hardee, Josh Allen, Marc "Ghost" Lawson, Tony Sanchez, Alyssa Lee, Ben Murray, John Burns, Mike Burns, John Hartsfield, Danny Robinson, Rita McClenny, Diane Bechamps, James Williams, Greg & Necole Simmonds, Chris Haynes, Ken Johnson, Jack Hartmann, William Rolack, Maurice Coleman, Sterling Roberson, Mark Szollar, Leo Gordon, Ron Ippolito, Principal Kara Backman, Vice Principal Genevieve Johnston, Kevin Atlas, Davina Leone, Keith Carter, Marvin Robinson, Lester Johnson, John Mayo, Kelli Lemon, Anoa Monsho, Michael Robinson, Caleb "Kaikor" Sawyer, Bill Dennis, Jennifer Reyes-White, Danielle Silverstein, John Warren Thompson, John & Wynn Thompson, Warren Barge, Paul Barge, Mark Wilkins, Tom & Delores Wilkins, Charles & Angela Pullen, Gabe Rein, Frank Edmonds, Lynn Edmonds, Chekeim Wymes, Doug Barrios, John Crane, George Charles, Django Degree, Reginia Brown-Hester, Richard Dunn, Elander Lewis, Steve Williams, Detavio Samuels, Eric Hutcherson, Natoya Brown, Jeff Woodton, Martin & Tamara Ekechukwu, Eternal Polk, Omar Johnson, Michael Prichard, Jim Kleverweis, Steve Jones, Joseph Grant, Pete Chatmon, Isha Sesay, Molly Dewolf Swenson, Reggie Rock Bythewood, Karen Horne, Ajamu Johnson, Ebonne Ruffins, Keesha Boyd, Steve Harris, Ben Tubuo, Rasheda Donner, Eric Covert, Ankit Brahmkshatri, Sonia Borris, Jay Roewe, Diane Fitzgerald, Cody Pike (photography) and Drew Dove (graphic design).

I want to thank everyone who has supported the Genius Factor Academy, the Make Your Passion Your Paycheck Course; and my public speaking/lecture series. I specifically want to thank the leadership at the California Association of Directors of Activities (CADA). I am extremely grateful to be part of the CADA preferred partners program and speakers bureau. Additionally, I want to thank Denair High School, Oak Hills High School, Walnut High School, and the United Federation of Teachers (UFT)- teachers' union in New York City.

Finally, I want to thank everyone who has bought this book. I take this platform and the opportunity to have a global impact on people very seriously, and I am eternally grateful for your support - THANK YOU! #MakeYourPassionYourPaycheck

Much Love,

Works Cited

G-Factor

Gardner, H. (1983). *Frames of mind: The theory of multiple intelligences*. New York: Basic Books.

Eurich, Tasha. 2018. "What Self-Awareness Really Is (and How to Cultivate It)." Harvard Business Review. January 4, 2018. https://hbr.org/2018/01/what-self-awareness-really-is-and-how-to-cultivate-it.

Passion to Paycheck Profiles

Michael Jordan

Jr, Tom Huddleston. 2020. "How Michael Jordan Became Great: 'Nobody Will Ever Work as Hard as I Work.'" CNBC. April 21, 2020. https://www.cnbc.com/2020/04/21/how-michael-jordan-became-great-nobody-will-ever-work-as-hard.html.

Stewart, Wayne. (2005). *The Little Giant Book of Basketball Facts*. New York: Sterling Publishing Company.

"Michael Jordan Net Worth 2021: What Is Jordan's Deal with Nike?" 2021. MARCA. October 17, 2021. https://www.marca.com/en/basketball/nba/2021/10/17/616c0df146163f846f8b45b5.html.

Tim Grover

Johnson, Chris. n.d. "How Tim Grover Became One of the NBA's Most Revered Trainers." Sports Illustrated. https://www.si.com/edge/2014/06/02/how-tim-grover-became-one-nbas-most-revered-trainers.

"About Tim Grover - ATTACK Athletics CEO and Best-Selling Author." 2017. Tim Grover. October 4, 2017. https://timgrover.com/about/.

Chloe Kim

Rosenberg, Michael. n.d. "Chloe Kim Stole the Show in 2018." Sports Illustrat-ed. Accessed January 21, 2022. https://www.si.com/olympics/2018/11/28/chloe-kim-winter-olympics-2018-sportsperson-top-moments.

"Kelly Clark Wins Superpipe, and Chloe Kim, 13, Earns Silver." 2014. The Denver Post. January 25, 2014. https://www.denverpost.com/2014/01/25/kelly-clark-wins-superpipe-and-chloe-kim-13-earns-silver/.

"Chloe Kim." 2016. Team USA. 2016. https://www.teamusa.org/us-ski-and-snowboard/athletes/Chloe-Kim.

Nicole Lynn

"Nicole Lynn and Agent You: Show Up, Do the Work and Succeed on Your Own Terms." n.d. Spreaker. Accessed January 21, 2022. https://www.spreaker.com/user/iamrefocusedpodcast/nicole-lynn-and-agent-you-show-up-do-the.

J.R. Gamble. 2019. "Nicole Lynn, a Groundbreaking Sports Agent Pioneer." The Shadow League. The Shadow League. April 25, 2019. https://theshadowleague.com/nicole-lynn-a-groundbreaking-sports-agent-pioneer/.

Lynn, Nicole. (2021) *Agent You: Show Up Do the Work and Succeed on Your Own Terms.* New York. HarperCollins.

Dr. Dre & Jimmy Iovine

Ramsay, Derek. 2017. "Jimmy Iovine." Variety. September 26, 2017. https://variety.com/exec/jimmy-iovine/.

Earl, C. F. *Dr. Dre.* September 2012. New York. Simon and Schuster.

"Dr Dre's Apple deal will make him the richest man in hip-hop." May 9, 2014. The Guardian.

LaFranco, Robert; Binelli, Mark; Goodman, Fred (June 13, 2002). "U2, Dre High-est Earning Artists". *Rolling Stone.*

John Williams

"John Williams Biography (1932-)." *Www.filmreference.com*, Filmreference.com/film/83/John-Williams.html. Accessed 21 Jan. 2022.

Billie Eilish

Rosenzweig, Mathias. (August 9, 2016) "Meet Billie Eilish, Pop's Next It Girl" *Vogue.*

"Billie Eilish." *GRAMMY.com*, 15 Dec. 2020, www.grammy.com/grammys/artists/billie-eilish/251741.

DJ Khaled

"DJ Khaled." *Biography*, 12 Nov. 2017, www.biography.com/musician/dj-khaled.

KAWS

"10 Things to Know about KAWS." 2019. Christies.com. Christies. October 30, 2019. https://www.christies.com/features/KAWS-artist-guide-9756-1.aspx.

Steve Ditko

Andy Lewis and Aaron Couch (July 6, 2018) "SteveDitko, Spider-Man Co-Creator and Legendary Comics Artist, Dies at 90." *Hollywood Reporter.*

Sunny Anderson

"BTU #269 - Air Force to Co-Host of Food Network's the Kitchen (Sunny Anderson)." *Beyond the Uniform*, beyondtheuniform.org/blog/btu-269-air-force-to-co-host-of-food-networks-the-kitchen-sunny-anderson. Accessed 21 Jan. 2022.

Virgil Abloh

Friedman, Vanessa. 2021. "Virgil Abloh Gets a Seat at the Power Table." *The New York Times*, July 20, 2021, sec. Style. https://www.nytimes.com/2021/07/20/style/virgil-abloh-lvmh-off-white.html.

Ninja

Montag, Ali. 2018. "How This 26-Year-Old Went from Working at a Fast Food Joint to Making $500,000 a Month Playing Video Games." CNBC. March 20, 2018. https://www.cnbc.com/2018/03/20/tyler-ninja-blevins-from-working-at-noodles-co-to-twitch-gamer.html.

Mark Zuckerberg

"Facebook Surges and Mark Zuckerberg Pockets $3.8 Billion." n.d. Finance. yahoo.com. Accessed January 21, 2022. https://finance.yahoo.com/blogs/daily-ticker/facebook-surges-mark-zuckerberg-pockets-3-8-billion-143114560.html.

Levy, Steven. (2020) *Facebook: The Inside Story.* New York, Blue Rider Press.

Morgan Debaun

"5 Black Business Leaders Who Are Changing the Face of Silicon Valley." n.d. Finance.yahoo.com. Accessed January 21, 2022. https://finance.yahoo.com/news/groundbreaking-business-leaders-silicon-valley-190329310.html.

"About." *Connect with Morgan DeBaun and Her World*, 9 Oct. 2020, morgandebaun.com/about2/. Accessed 21 Jan. 2022.

Tristan Walker

McCorvey, J.J. (December 12, 2018). "Tristan Walker announces acquisition by Procter & Gamble, will remain as CEO and move company to Atlanta." *FastCompany.*

"Bloomberg - Are You a Robot?" n.d. www.bloomberg.com. Accessed January 21, 2022. https://www.bloomberg.com/features/2016-how-did-i-get-here/tristan-walker.html.

Oprah

Kelley, Kelly. (2010). *Oprah: A Biography.* New York. Three Rivers Press.

Haynes, Clarence. "Oprah Winfrey: All the Ways the First Black Female Billionaire Has Made History." *Biography*, 31 Jan. 2019, www.biography.com/news/oprah-winfrey-achievements.

Charlie D'Amelio

Brown, Abram. n.d. "TikTok's 7 Highest-Earning Stars: New Forbes List Led by Teen Queens Addison Rae and Charli D'Amelio." Forbes. Accessed January 21, 2022. https://www.forbes.com/sites/abrambrown/2020/08/06/tiktoks-highest-earning-stars-teen-queens-addison-rae-and-charli-damelio-rule/?sh=5c9198815087.

Gary V.

Vaynerchuk, Gary. (2010) *Crush It!: Why NOW Is the Time to Cash In on Your Passion.* New York. HaperCollins.

Vaynerchuk, Gary. "Gary Vaynerchuk." *GaryVaynerchuk.com*, 2009, www.garyvaynerchuk.com/biography/.

Horch, A. J. 2019. "Serial Entrepreneur Gary Vaynerchuk Reveals the Investment Secret That Made Him Millions." CNBC. May 30, 2019.

https://www.cnbc.com/2019/05/30/gary-vaynerchuk-reveals-the-investment-secret-that-made-him-millions.html.

Casey Neistat

Frankel, Daniel, and Daniel Frankel. "HBO Nabs the Neistats." *Variety*, 19 Mar. 2009, variety.com/2009/scene/markets-festivals/hbo-nabs-the-neistats-1118001386/. Accessed 21 Jan. 2022.

Jones, Dylan (September 22, 2016). "Why Casey Neistat is our New Media Star Of The Year. *GQ UK*.

Ryan Coogler

Connley, Courtney. "How 'Black Panther' Director Ryan Coogler Went from Living in His Car to Becoming Marvel's Youngest Filmmaker." *CNBC*, 23 Feb. 2018, www.cnbc.com/2018/02/23/ryan-coogler-became-marvels-youngest-filmmaker-with-black-panther.html.

Kroll, Justin. (July 24, 2013). "'Fruitvale Station' Team Eyeing 'Rocky' Spin-Off 'Creed' With MGM." *Variety*.

Lena Waithe

Kroll, Justin, and Justin Kroll. 2018. "Jodie Turner-Smith to Star Opposite Daniel Kaluuya in 'Queen & Slim' (EXCLUSIVE)." Variety. November 8, 2018. https://variety.com/2018/film/news/ jodie-smith-turner-queen-and-slim-daniel-kaluuya-1203022499/.

"Master of None's Lena Waithe: 'If You Come from a Poor Background, TV Becomes What You Dream About.'" 2018. The Guardian. January 5, 2018. https://www.theguardian.com/tv-and-radio/2018/jan/05/master-of-nones-lena-waithe-if-you-come-from-a-poor-background-tv-becomes-what-you-dream-about.

Stan Lee

"Story of Stan Lee - Article - Historydraft." *Historydraft.com*, historydraft.com/ story/stan-lee/article/703. Accessed 21 Jan. 2022.

J.K. Rowling

Rowling, J.K. 2016. "J.K. Rowling - J.K. Rowling." J.K. Rowling. 2016. https:// www.jkrowling.com/about/.

Hoffower, Hillary. n.d. "J.K. Rowling Is Worth at Least $670 Million, Though Some Say She's a Billionaire. Take a Look at How the Controversial Author Makes and Spends Her Fortune." Business Insider. https://www.businessinsider. com/jk-rowling-net-worth-spending-harry-potter-2020-6.

Jessamyn Stanley

Kerwin, Ann Marie (September 25, 2017). "The Beyoncé Effect". *Advertising Age*.

"Influencers Work out for U by Kotex Fitness | WARC." *Origin.warc.com*, www. warc.com/newsandopinion/news/influencers_work_out_for_u_by_kotex_fitness/40572. Accessed 21 Jan. 2022.

"About – Jessamyn Stanley." *Jessamynstanley.com*, jessamynstanley.com/ about/. Accessed 21 Jan. 2022.

Blake Mycoskie

Mycoskie, Blake. (2011). *Start something that matters*. New York: Spiegel & Grau.

Tony Robbins

O'Keefe, Brian. (October 30, 2014). Tony Robbins, "The CEO Whisperer." *Fortune*.

Michael Todd

Todd, Michael. (April 2020). Relationship Goals: How to Win at Dating, Marriage, and Sex. New York. WaterBrook.

"About Us | Transformation Church." n.d. https://transformchurch.us/aboutus/.

Jay Shetty

"Jay Shetty | Home." n.d. Jay Shetty. https://jayshetty.me/.

"Jay Shetty." n.d. Forbes. Accessed January 21, 2022. https://www.forbes.com/ profile/jay-shetty/?sh=32db5bb74f66.

DeSantis, Rachel, Charlotte Triggs November 19, and 2019 11:22 Am. n.d. "Meet Jay Shetty, the Motivational Vlogger and Ex-Monk Who Has Fans in the Kardashians & Ellen DeGeneres." PEOPLE.com. https://people.com/ human-interest/meet-jay-shetty-motivational-vlogger-ex-monk/.

Warren Buffett

Bloomberg.com. n.d. "Bloomberg Billionaires Index." https://www.bloomberg. com/billionaires/profiles/warren-e-buffett/.

"Who Is Warren Buffett?" n.d. Coinspeaker. Accessed January 21, 2022. https:// www.coinspeaker.com/persons/warren-buffett/.

Investing, Full Bio Follow Twitter Joshua Kennon co-authored "The Complete Idiot's Guide to, 3rd Edition, and runs his own asset management firm for the affluent Read The Balance's editorial policies Joshua Kennon. n.d. "Warren

Buffet: One of the Wealthiest People in America." The Balance. https://www.thebalance.com/warren-buffett-timeline-356439.

Robert Smith

Smith Contributor, By Robert F. n.d. "Robert F. Smith." Forbes. Accessed January 21, 2022. https://www.forbes.com/profile/robert-f-smith/?list=forbes-400&sh=19dfd1fd2236.

Katherine Johnson

Shetterly, Margot. 2020. "Katherine Johnson Biography." NASA. February 24, 2020. https://www.nasa.gov/content/katherine-johnson-biography.

Neil DeGrasse Tyson

"Neil DeGrasse Tyson." 2018. Biography. January 19, 2018. https://www.biography.com/scientist/neil-degrasse-tyson.

Al Gore

"Nobel Prize Summit." n.d. NobelPrize.org. Accessed January 21, 2022. https://www.nobelprize.org/events/nobel-prize-summit/2021/panellists/al-gore/.

Jaden Smith:

"About." n.d. JUST WATER. https://justwater.com/pages/about.

Locker, Melissa. 2019. "Jaden Smith's Just Water Just Hit $100 Million Valuation." Fast Company. September 4, 2019. https://www.fastcompany.com/90398045/jaden-smiths-just-water-just-hit-100-million-valuation.

Matt Damon

"About Water.org - Learn about Our Water NGO | Water.org." 2009. Water.org. 2009. https://water.org/about-us/.

About the Authors

Torrance Hampton is a seasoned director, executive producer, writer, and brand strategist with a track record of developing successful consumer-centric campaigns for luxury, sports, and lifestyle entertainment brands. He is the founder, creative director, and executive producer for G|FACTOR FILMS, a multicultural brand strategy and storytelling collective that works with some of the world's most influential brands, including Walt Disney Motion Picture Studios, Nickelodeon, LEGO, Universal Music Group, NFL, NBA, BET, REVOLT TV, Comcast/NBC Universal, Xfinity Black Experience, Bentley Motors, Aston Martin, and Nextdoor. After finding great success in the business world as a passionate storyteller, Torrance is now actively developing original content (scripted & non-scripted) as well as mentoring, inspiring and educating the next generation of leaders. His core beliefs are that everyone is a genius and that everyone has genius-level talent. Through his entrepreneurial journey, he has realized that self-awareness, emotional intelligence (EQ), identifying your passion, and activating your Genius Factor are the catalysts to a life of happiness and success. To book Torrance for speaking engagements or to inquire about his online career exploration course, please visit www.torrancehampton.com.

TEXT 917-540-3352 to continue the conversation with Torrance and join the Global Genius Factor Community.

Christina Morgan is a writer and editor who lives in Brooklyn, New York. She has worked for HarperCollins Publishers and Houghton Mifflin Harcourt.

MAKE YOUR PASSION
YOUR PAYCHECK ™

MEME GENERATOR